Earlham

Percy Lubbock

Printing Statement:

Due to the very old age and scarcity of this book,
many of the pages may be hard to read due to the
blurring of the original text, possible missing pages,
missing text, dark backgrounds and other issues
beyond our control.

Because this is such an important and rare work, we
believe it is best to reproduce this book regardless of
its original condition.

Thank you for your understanding.

Earlham

Percy Lubbock

Author of *The Craft of Fiction*

Jonathan Cape
Eleven Gower Street London

First Published November 1922.
Second Impression November 1922.
Third Impression December 1922.
All Rights Reserved.

CONTENTS

v

EARLHAM

EARLHAM

I: INDOORS

I

THE slightest turn of memory takes me back at any time to Earlham, to the big sunny hall where we used to assemble for morning prayers. The shallow staircase descended on one side, by the great front-door. Opposite to it another door opened to the garden, and through two wide windows, tangled with roses and vines, the sunshine welled into the house. The hall was broad and square, rather bare of furniture; against the walls there were seats, velveted and fringed, once of a strong old crimson, but now faded away into soft rose-leaf colours under the suns of many summers; there was a round table, where our grandfather sat with his large Bible. At prayer-time there were also benches, set out in rows, for the servants who came filing in through a swing-door in one corner. First the stout little bright-eyed cook, whose place was next to the garden-door —she carefully shut it against the dewy morning air if it happened to stand open; then the rest of the household in due order. It struck us as an imposing procession; from our red seats under the windows we looked across and watched it streaming and streaming through the swing-door, from the back-region of the house.

EARLHAM

Prayers began with an unaccompanied hymn. Our grandmother, standing before the wide chimney, struck into the first notes, with a little toss of her lace-capped head—lifted up her singularly sweet and resonant voice, and the rest of us followed in unison. She sang, in her old age, with a voice as fresh as a girl's, soaring and pealing with perfect ease; and her voice had a quality that I never seem to have heard in another, clear and vivid and plangent, like some kind of silver-wired harp. She soared into the melody quite at random, with no thought of the pitch; and sometimes it was a trying one for the congregation, and after the first verse she would cry "A little lower," and start the second verse in a more tenable key. She sang from the heart, and the words of the hymn (soundly evangelical) floated upon the melody, dominating it, *using* it, so that the tune became a real accompaniment to the words. Our repertory was not greatly varied; but often and often as the same familiar song was repeated—" Hark my soul," perhaps, or " Jesu stand among us "—she would utter the words of praise and thanksgiving with a thrill, a radiant conviction, as though she made them her own for the first time.

Meanwhile our grandfather sat at his round table, one hand propping the bald dome of his forehead, the other arm embracing the big Bible that lay before him. He took no part in the hymn, he waited; and when we were seated he read the chapter over which he had been brooding. And then there was a pause, and we settled ourselves anew, and a tract of time opened before us that

2

seemed very long indeed; it had no measurable length, like a hymn or a chapter, for it depended on our grandfather alone. There was first a commentary upon the passage he had read; he talked of it, I suppose he would explain and expound it; but what do I know?—it was a time that passed for me in a methodical scrutiny of the assembly, our dear and well-known friends of the household, ranged on their benches, our uncles and cousins on the red settees. Presently the arm that embraced the Bible began slowly, slowly to close it, and the exposition was at an end, and we knelt; and then there was nothing to do but to wait, helping oneself out with a little rhythmical fidgeting.

Our grandfather, fervently, appealingly, lyrically, delivered a long improvisation of prayer. All of it is lost to me, save for an occasional landmark that I could recognize and appreciate as it passed; such were topical points, special invocations on behalf of members of the family, often ourselves, who had just arrived or were about to depart. Otherwise it is all vague; but I can hear the warm, mild old voice rising and falling with intonations like an autumn wind—or like the chant, as it strikes me now, of a minstrel of the family roof-tree, a voice soaring and sinking in slightly melancholy cadences, while it lingers over a half-extemporized, half-traditional lay. It was always a wonder to us —we had no other reflection upon the matter—that our grandfather could uplift his eloquence afresh on every morning of the year, with never a lapse or a hesitation; but it ran on lines long established, I imagine, as the eloquence of a bard over the glories

3

of the past. It was certainly in its manner the voice of poetry. The minutes lengthened; and at last the voice rose in a familiar climax and fell on the words (always the same) " We ask it—in the name of— " and presently we were all joining in the Lord's Prayer, a goodly volume of sound, with the fervour of tension relieved. A last blessing, a pause, and the stir of life began again.

2

In due course the genial red-bearded butler pounded the gong, and breakfast was ready in the big outlying dining-room. That was a room that had been added some generations before, when the house was already venerable; it was built out at an angle to the old body of the house, and it had a bow-window at one end, facing into the flower-beds on the edge of the great lawn, and other windows looking over the side-lawn, to the west, and down the slope of the park to the river. Mirth-making, free-tongued parties were constantly seen round the long table; a child, squeezing and craning between two elders after grapes and peaches, would be amazed and enchanted by the light jesting brilliance that played round the company. Indeed the family of our grandparents was rich in its vein of jovial comedy Our uncles were terribly amusing, so free with each other, so wicked with their parents. One could stare and listen; and I remember the heady feeling of importance when one was personally addressed, and perhaps the hot confusion when the laugh turned upon oneself.

They were mornings of perfect and lovely

romance, and well we knew it at the time. Earlham days were holidays, Earlham was the wonder of the world. And indeed it was a beautiful old house, red and mellow, spacious, sun-bathed. There were gables of flint and brick with a date on them, 1642, which I suppose marked the earliest core of the building. But later on, perhaps in the reign of Queen Anne, the older building had been all but swallowed up in a house with a big garden-front, to the south, and rows of high sash-windows, and two projecting wings to the north that reached out and enclosed you as you arrived, as you drove up in the family carriage, palpitating with excitement, to the semi-circle of steps before the front-door. The carriage made a sweep and a curve, and the coach-man on the box seized the handle of a bell that hung on the wall of the house, at the right height for his hand—seized it as the carriage swept round, pealed it, and the big door was already opening as we drew up at the steps. Our grandfather would be standing there, tall and gaunt and benevolent; that was how the visit to Earlham began.

The north front had been plastered and painted a buff-white, long ago; but elsewhere the red brick was untouched, only the vines and roses and jessa-mine clung and scrambled where they would. Late in the eighteenth century there had been more building, and the dining-room stood out into the garden, as I have said; and also to the west, where there was the view down to the river, another wing was thrown forward, with a drawing-room that faced away to the sunset, and to the glint of water, and to the round tower of Colney church on the rising ground beyond, a mile away. So the house had gradually elbowed itself into convenient roominess. The back-regions, too, through the swing-door, were extremely interesting. A flagged passage led away to the back-door, and there before it was a large green of rough grass, and round it all the outlying buildings that in old days had been part of the needful economy of the place, the store-houses, the bakery, the brew-house. In one corner, under a sort of brick cloister, was the pump—a great beam that revolved, and that for half an hour every morning was dragged round and round by a white horse, with a measured thumping and thudding. By the back-door was the kitchen-window, and the kitchen was a noble room. From within the house you approached it by another flagged passage, out of which a side-door opened—or rather it was always locked, till the rosy cook drew a key from her pocket, opened the door, and there was a waft of sweet dry spiciness from her stores, while she searched among them for something to content us.

The house was various, endless, inexhaustible. Mounting the stairs again (after how many years?), the shallow stairs that rose from the hall, I hardly know which way to turn—here, perhaps, on the first landing, at a door which takes me into the " ante-room," I suppose originally the chief parlour. It was high, clear, formal, with the air of a room little used; there was not an object on a table, not a blue china cup on a cabinet, that had shifted its place in fifty years. But at the end of the long room was a small extension, a projection in a bow-window,

6

that was in familiar use. A cool green light fell through the windows, which looked northward into an avenue of great limes, murmurous and odorous in summer noondays; and our grandmother would gather us to this end of the room, the coolest retreat in the house, in the heat of the long brilliant day. The space in the bow-window was raised like a dais above the level of the room; there was a green velvet window-seat, and a huge old Chinese jar, standing on the floor, holding relics of ancestral lavender and rose-leaves. There on the window-seat our grandmother drew us round her and read to us, sweetly and playfully, ancient moral anecdotes, stories out of tiny little volumes that she cherished—or Bible-stories, if it were Sunday. She read with a charming, trilling liveliness, dropping into soft mysterious undertones, breaking out again with silvery merriment—she had her own way in everything she did.

She loved the green window-seat and the rustling shadow of the limes. As she grew old and older, she used to sit there in the window for long hours, alone in the summer evening, till the light faded away. She sat without book or work, drinking in the twilit fragrance, communing in her mind—with what?—with the thought of many beloved dead, whom she had lost and mourned, and with the joy of reunion with them that she saw near at hand now, in a very few years. Her mind was *there*, more and more. As the evening darkened she seemed, sitting in the window, to have all but passed already into the light she awaited; it shone in her face, I remember, as she spoke of it; I remember vividly her look as she once exclaimed, in sudden uncontrollable wonder, " *What* will it be ?—what will it be like ? " So close to it she felt herself to be, so near the inconceivable and ineffable; the wonder of anticipation held and filled her.

3

She liked us to love the old house, as we did; she was very tender and affectionate with it, as though the house were a kind old nurse, faithful and worn, with whom we must be gentle. She would lay her hand on a wall, a panel, a window-sill, with a touch that seemed to stroke it softly; " the poor old place," she said, with a kind of bantering tenderness. She lived there for nearly fifty years, and her many children grew up there. Nothing was ever changed. The house had been all new-furnished when she went to live there, a few years after her first marriage, and so it remained. Wandering through the rooms again, at this late day, I suppose I can note how inharmoniously, unsuitably, the house had been treated; there was little or nothing in the dressing and fitting of the rooms that might seem to accord with the grace of age, to suggest a memory akin to the house. The house had the memory of a high style, there was none in its furnishing. But crimson had faded to rose, green to the colour of autumn grasses and moss, and in the drawing-room (through the mahogany door from the ante-room) the yellow satin of the window-hangings had a faint gleam of old amber. Three windows there were, slightly bowed out to the west; and we are now, you understand, on the first floor of the house.

INDOORS

Through one of the three drawing-room windows, that to the right hand, there was an unexpected glimpse. A rather dense shrubbery or small wood of oaks stood in that quarter, flanking close against the house; but a clearance was tunnelled through it and kept open, aligned with this window; and a view appeared there, framed in greenery, of a bridge, a round brick arch, that spanned the river down by the village. It made a neat little picture, like an old drawing-master's copy. And if you remember a page near the beginning of Lavengro, where Borrow goes fishing in a river-pool, by a bridge, and falls in with a handsome Quaker gentleman in a broad beaver hat, who mildly rebukes him for his occupation and talks to him of the Scriptures—this is that same bridge, the good Quaker was our great-grand-father's brother, Joseph John Gurney, who lived at Earlham before our grandmother's day. Borrow wandered out to the Earlham river, after his fishing, from Norwich, and Joseph John, strolling down through the park, found him and gently catechized him, and invited him to come up to the house and see his books—where Borrow went, however, only in after years, and was then entertained by the good man in a " low quiet chamber, whose one window, shaded by a gigantic elm, looks down the slope towards the pleasant stream "; and it must be admitted that there was no such room in the house, nor any " gigantic elm " in the garden at all. But Borrow fished in the pool and talked to Joseph John and visited the house, no doubt—the " Earl's Home," as he calls it; and this was his bridge that appeared in its round frame of leafy foreground.

Joseph John was a handsome old scholar and philanthropist and man of business, mildly literary. His portrait remained at Earlham, a head of distinction, with kind lucid eyes. More interesting was a picture that hung in the drawing-room, a large water-colour, in a frame with folding doors to it—a portrait by Richmond of a Quaker lady, old and portly and immensely majestic, in mob-cap and flowing robe of soft brown and grey. This was Aunt Fry, sister of Joseph John—Elizabeth Fry, missionary of the prison-house, recalled and commemorated still for her fruitful works. She was much more commanding, much more resolute, I judge, than her brother; she looked as though she had accomplished her good works with a high hand; and mixed with legitimate pride in her fame, there survived in the family some tradition that she was more interested in her grand European activities than in her nearest and homeliest duties. She had lived at Earlham in her youth, with her many brothers and sisters; and she became a character that perhaps, to her family circle, seemed strangely public; and in our grandmother's voice, as she spoke to us of Aunt Fry, there might be a hint of such an idea, quickly covered with admiring veneration.

Aunt Fry hung in a corner of the room, looking very stately. But I cannot think of her just yet, for my eye has been caught elsewhere. Near the windows stood the " instrument," a grand piano in golden satin-wood, and there the assault of memory is strong and manifold. It was a ghostly piano; the music came softly tinkling out of it with a

muffled sound, as though it were swathed in veils of
time. You could not stir it up or rouse it to more
than a far-away hum and murmur; thumping
and strumming had no effect, it only responded with
the same low shadowy voice. Our grandmother,
we believed, used to play it and sing songs when she
was young; in our day she never touched it, and
her voice was only heard in hymn-singing at prayers
and in church. But yes, once I heard her sing out
to the sound of the piano, as with an echo of her
youth. Somebody was touching the keys and
turning over a book of old songs, sentimental old
ballads mostly, but he found some music there of
Handel and Arne. Presently, turning another page,
he played a few notes of a song, and named it, and
asked our grandmother if she had ever sung it;
and as she moved about the room she turned and
shook out the first phrase of the song, suddenly,
with her bright harp-tones—" Nita, Juanita!"
The phrase rang across the room, it is still in my
ears; it was a flash of old times, when the voice
of the piano was young and clear too, perhaps.
The piano had aged and lost its voice; but to those
ringing notes of " Nita, Juanita " it might have
responded, finding the tone of its youth again.

It couldn't do that; but still it tinkled industri-
ously, and the children gazed into its gaping jaws
to watch the dance of the little black hammers. We
sang all the sentimental ballads, The Captive
Knight, The Hebrew Maiden to her Christian Lover,
Oh Pilot 'tis a Fearful Night, many more. Our
grandmother, hearing us, would come in and stand
listening for a moment, nodding and smiling to us.

" Ah, those droll old songs! " she would say. But she was not sentimental herself; she looked back lightly and gaily to the far past, I think. She lived vividly in the present, full of quick impulses and melting sympathies. I have spoken of her as I saw her just now, sitting in the twilight; but that is a picture which only belongs to the last years, the very last. Till then did we ever see her sitting still, resting, waiting? She was always in movement, she had remembered someone she wished to see, something she had forgotten, something she had lost. She smiled and waved to us, seeing us happily occupied, and was gone.

Nobody ever " sat " in the drawing-room by day, there was no company there till the evening. And while the company was at dinner, one of the children would follow our well-beloved Rose, the house-maid, as she went her round—first to the bed-rooms, to fold away the counterpanes and turn down the sheets of the huge four-posters, then to the drawing-room, to set the chairs and brighten the lamps, and if there was a dinner-party to open the " instrument " and light the candles. " There's company to-night, they'll be having some music." We prepared the room for them and whisked out of the way; Rose somehow made a drama of the proceeding. Bright and merry and handsome she was, carrying her head high—a charming figure, as we slipped round the turn of the stairs, hearing the voices of the company as they issued confusedly from the dining-room, away in the distance.

INDOORS

4

Lingering still by the drawing-room window, I come on another picture. It is of a child, who sits there in the window-seat, gazing, gaping, while someone—a kind lady, unknown—tells him a story. There was some kind of tea-party proceeding in the room, apparently—which was very unusual, and I guess it may have been a missionary meeting, with an address and a collection, and tea to follow. Anyhow there were people crowding and talking around; but the child was hardly aware of them, he was all eyes and open mouth at the kind lady's story. Not a word of it do I remember, save only that the climax was a house on fire, I suppose with a gallant rescue of the inmates. The story-teller sat beside me in the window-seat, her friendly eyes in mine; and she must have felt pleased at the success of her tale. It was surely suitable and interesting, the very story for a child—no doubt she had told it to scores. I wonder who she was; she little suspected how I was to pay for that story. The fiery house, the flames shooting from the windows, must have happened to press upon some sensitive spot in a small imagination, straining or wounding it. The memory became a dread, a monstrosity, that haunted me for long—for years, as it seems to me now. It began with that session in the window-seat, in the greyish evening light, when a kind stranger took the trouble to entertain a child.

It began there, and it returned, night after night, in the room where the children slept. That indeed was an odd and disconcerting room for the calmest imagination. The Eleven-sided Room—so it was called, and there was no doubt about its eleven distinct walls and angles; we often counted them. It might have represented the space which the builder happened to find upon his hands, when he had provided the other rooms in their order. It was full of slopes and projections, recesses, yawning cupboards like caves. An extemporized wooden staircase had been pierced to the nursery below; and there was another door that opened on to a deserted and resonant upper landing, and there were more doors that concealed strange alcoves; and between them you felt utterly exposed and powerless. You could not watch them all, you could not be on your guard in all directions at once. A candle on the mantel-piece gave just enough light to show how dark the corners were. The long hours were urgent with horror—surely half the night had gone, surely it must be near the dawn; yet still there was the sound of plates and forks and voices in the nursery below—far away, in the world of company and light, at the foot of the wooden staircase—and our nurse was still at her supper, gossiping with our grandmother's dear affectionate maid. Down there was security and peace, and tender hearts, moreover, that would have been lavished to protect and comfort a frightened child, if only—if only they could be made to understand. But alone up there among the shadows, how could you make them understand? Where could you begin with any explanation? It was hopeless; but perhaps there were feints and ruses that might bring one of them up the wooden stairs, and a few minutes of safe company might be secured in that way. Sometimes it could be managed, but not often, and not for long. Silence, solitude must be faced, and the blaze of that horrible house, with the flames leaping from its window-sockets as soon as one's eyes were shut. Hours and hours dragged on, the dawn delayed.

The soft roo-hooing of pigeons on the roof, a great splash of sun slanting through the window, life and freedom and daylight were all around one in a moment. It was another room, another world in the morning. The caverns and recesses were stimulating and amusing; the Eleven-sided Room was unique, entirely delicious. The clean old smell of sun-baked woodwork met one at the windows, which were fringed with green leaves. Bumping presently down the stairs, to breakfast in the nursery below, one set forth upon the illimitable day. The nursery was high and bare, but the sun filled it. Only a four-sided room it was, like any other, but it had five doors, five separate entrances. Through one of them we clattered off along the passage, when the gong boomed for prayers.

5

Our grandfather, infinitely kind and mild, was yet not easily approachable. He was very tall and lean; he towered above you, he looked down from his height benignantly, but with nothing in particular to say. Under his high forehead his eyes were remote and cavernous; his thin cheeks were drawn together to the point of his chin. He twinkled in silent approval and passed on like a shadow; he seemed to walk in twilight. He did not join the talkative, sociable party; he glanced in upon it, gleaming for a moment with appreciation, answering a gay challenge with a chuckle and a word, and stalked away. We saw him, tall and black, walking across the great lawn, not loitering or pausing, but like a practised walker (as he was), with a measured and regular pace that was neither a stride nor a stroll; his big substantial boots rose and fell steadily, and he covered the ground in surprising time, without appearing to hurry himself. Or on the lawn, perhaps, he would sometimes pause, to drive the point of his umbrella under a plantain or a dandelion. And then he was off on his three-mile trudge along the high-road to Norwich, where in old days (before my memory) he had been rector of a city parish, and where many missions of charity or clerical business always called him.

He had been rector of St. Giles's, in Norwich, for many years, tramping in perpetually from Earlham and out again. But I scarcely look back further than the time when he resigned his populous cure in the city, having accomplished a great work there, and took instead the diminutive living of Earlham itself, with the village of Colney that adjoined it. At Earlham Hall he had lived since his marriage (he was really our *step*-grandfather), and now he ministered in the two tiny churches, Earlham and Colney, turn and turn about. Living at the Hall himself, he used to lend his rectory-house to stray and stranded missionaries—I think they were generally missionaries. From China, from Uganda they came and were harboured in the pretty old

16

rectory of Colney, with their wives and children, for the term of their holiday. Many threads of friendship radiated from Earlham into the mission-field, all round the world.

But I cannot write of our grandfather as though I were telling his story; I can only watch for glimpses of him, seizing them where I can, and our glimpses of him in those days appear like the passing of a benevolent shadow, always excepting the sight of him at prayers and in church. There only, I now see, we could look into his real life; he opened his mind in prayer and revealed the ardent emotion upon which his life was fed; at other times it was veiled and withdrawn, unsuspected by a child. We did not approach him familiarly; though nothing could seem more familiar to me now than the sight of him, as we loiter and cluster about the garden-door after prayers—the sight of him passing through the chatter and laughter with a demure, roguish smile, walking off in the sunshine among the brilliant flower-beds that skirted the lawn, returning presently with a single flower, a rose, for the tiny glass upon his writing-table. His study was by the garden-door; loitering outside, we could see him moving within among the high book-shelves. He was, or he had been, a student and a scholar, and his room had a refined, faded, scrupulous look, like the college-rooms of an old-fashioned don. Nothing unkempt, nothing haphazard; there was an air, rather, of remote traditional elegance, a kind of far-away nattiness; in college rooms of the old style, reaching back beyond the days of tobacco-smoke, beyond the days of lounging and sprawling, I have found something of that atmosphere. A room had naturally, like its owner, to be well-mannered and trimly appointed; it was impossible to imagine our grandfather in any but seemly, orderly surroundings.

He had not, however, what are called the "manners of the old school"; he was not courtly, not ceremonious; he was simple and kind and grave, as he talked to the stranger at his table—or talked not much, or not at all, if the conversation flowed freely around him. And indeed it flowed freely at that table—can I recall the bountiful board in the long dining-room without the crackle of our uncles' humour, genially unafraid and unashamed? Smiling discreetly over his carving at the head of the table, our grandfather withdrew from the talk, but missed none of it.

Mr. Jones, perhaps, or Mr. Smith, reverend gentlemen, bearded and hearty, would surely be seated at that table, as I think of it. There were plenty of reverend gentlemen there, doubtless of all complexions—but the beards predominated, the jovial wagging beards of evangelical country clergy. I wonder whether the children at the table, staring and listening, absorbing so much more than they knew, may not have acquired from these gentry their earliest notion of clerical institutions and categories—simple enough, in Mr. Jones's view. In our family we heard nothing of the " church "; our grandparents never used the word, as it seems to me; " church " only meant Earlham church next Sunday, Colney the Sunday after; prayer and

18

thanksgiving, love and praise were all the words we heard. But for Mr. Jones and his like there was more; there was something in the air of their talk that was quite unlike the air of Earlham. Surely we were conscious of that; for from nothing in our own circle could we have derived a knowledge of bad people, wrong and perverted and dangerous—ritualists, they were called. Our grandfather, indeed, could speak sharply about them; but these bad people would never have been spoken of or heard of, I think, but for Mr. Jones and his friends. *They* spoke of them, quite readily.

We knew all about the ritualists and their bad ways, and the " High Church Party," and so forth; but these matters could not be taken over-seriously, where our uncles made free with the talk. I quite understood the delicious impudence of one of them (the youngest, the most shameless, the one of all that company who was to vanish first, mourned untimely), when he called out his ribaldry at Mr. Jones across the table. I can clearly see that particular greybeard—large, jocose, loudly enjoying his good meal; from a neighbouring country parish he had lately moved to some living at Cromer or Lowestoft. " Mr. Jones," cried our uncle, dimpling with effrontery, " I suppose, now that you've gone to a fashionable church at the sea-side, you've become terribly *ritualistic!* " Oh the gay pugnacious whoop of Mr. Jones—can you hear it? " What, what, what? What's this? " " Oh yes, Mr. Jones, I expect you've become a sad Roman." Bursting and bubbling with rich indignant playfulness, Mr. Jones snorted and trumpeted; and our grandfather's smile would broaden as he carved the joint.

6

From the dining-room, from the company and the quality, the children would go bounding into the other world, the domestic household. Racing along the flagged passage to the kitchen, perhaps— or up the echoing backstairs to the top of the house, the spacious attics and landings, store-rooms and linen-presses—wherever they went they found delight. All over the house there was the same free wash of light and air, and a fragrance of clean wood, homely soap, fresh linen; the upper passages were bare and carpetless, full of echoes in the long stretches of scrubbed boards. The children had the right that only children possess—the freedom of both worlds, upstairs and downstairs, the attic and the parlour; at home with the merry servants as liberally as with the life below. Only children quite bridge that interval; they alone live naturally in both communities.

The household community at Earlham was brilliant and irresistible. It was all bright faces, good talk, interesting employment; year by year we were gathered in afresh and welcomed back to a world that seemed never to know change. We dropped into it, we made free of it to the point of being an embarrassment at times, I surely think. If we were we never suspected it, nor had reason to do so. But is it pleasant, when you are marshalling your forces for the dishing of a dinner—when you are sweeping, dusting, washing, mending—is it pleasant, when you are busy and responsible, to be

beset by young idleness in knickerbockers, appealed
to, clung to, danced with by irresponsibility in a
pinafore, at any time, all times? Always busy,
always patient, always gay and brilliant with a
sparkling of humour and originality, that household
lives in memory. Let affection, gratitude, admiration, be joined in a greeting to them.

The hall (*the* hall, as distinguished from the
" front hall ") was a fine place, almost collegiate,
with its long table, its high ceiling, its trophies on
the wall. Into the pantry that opened from it a
child would hardly venture; not that welcome
would fail, but because the world of the pantry is
excessively distinguished and experienced; and in
our attachment to our admirable friend, the red-
bearded butler, there is always mingled a touch of
dread. Of dread, do I really mean?—dread of our
genial friend? Well, there was a crisp ironic edge
to his words and looks, and such a free and masterful style about him as he strode through the hall
(the " front hall ") with the plates and the great
silver dish-covers to the dining-room, and as he
drummed on the gong at arm's length, with a
military action, and as he fired out of the pantry
window a brisk remark (with just that delightful
suspicion of the Norfolk drawl) to the coachman or
the gardener at the back-door. He was a man of the
world, that was it; no doubt one felt very young
with him. One grew a little older, perhaps, in the
course of years, and in unofficial hours he could be a
companion, immensely resourceful, on the river, on
a birds'-nesting excursion—such days I recall, when
we seemed to move upon the same level. But his

level in general was far above one's own; he was a man of mark. See him especially on days when he was in his element, when our grandmother was entertaining a few of her friends—a couple of hundred old souls from the work-house, say, or an army of school-children, swarming over the garden; he was in command and control of the situation. He did not particularly stoop, indeed, to their gossip or sport; I fancy him always surveying our grandmother's poor things with that amused, sardonic light in his eye; friendly, but briskly so, without effusion of sentiment. But the success of the occasion was in his hands, and it was safe; he organized and directed, and nothing that he handled went amiss. Every one who knew Earlham knew that man, and honoured him. He was the very faithful friend of our grandparents.

Round about the pantry window and the back-door there was a stir of life, in the morning hours, of which I always recapture the sense in reading of country-houses in the eighteenth century, and the routine of the old isolated, largely self-supporting village-mansion. Of course in our day there were punctual carts of tradesmen from Norwich, and the butler no longer brewed in the brew-house, and the rambling offices and dependencies of the old mansion were mostly deserted. But there they still were, and about the back-door and the flagged lobby with its benches within, there seemed to linger a tradition of another century. You found something like the sociable centre of a community there, you saw the substructure of an ancient establishment; the tradesman's cart had not completely replaced it with our more hand-to-mouth, more improvised manner of existence. A stable-boy brought the white horse to turn the pump; the gardener, the coachman, the keeper tramped in and out. Can I ever have seen a pedlar undoing a bale of finery and gimcrackery at that door, with the maids clustering round him? I have seen such an incident, or heard of it—and the difference between seeing and hearing is so slight to a child.

There certainly was one clear note of the *ancien régime* never wanting by the back-door. The halt, the maimed, the needy were invariably there; no modern rule that you must not " give to beggars " was ever recognized at Earlham. As I pass along the fresh-smelling dark passage to the flagged entry, I seem to know of two figures that I shall assuredly find there. One is the gardener, who stands before a table on which are arranged all the vases and jars and flower-stands from all the sitting-rooms; from a basket beside him he fills them with an incredible mixture of purple dahlias, red geraniums, orange marigolds, plumes of asparagus. And inevitably behind him, on the bench against the wall, ignored by the gardener (a grim man) but undiscouraged, sits the " poor man "—who has walked from Norwich to the fountain of charity, ever unsealed, that flows for all the needy at Earlham.

I believe the good butler, no sentimentalist, used to intercept the most shameless, protecting our grandmother from the continual assault upon her benevolence, so far as he could. It was a poor chance for a professional cadger when Sidell was first upon the scene; he would come marching down the passage with a bland business-like air, entirely proof against mere spectacular woes. But how often our grandmother was successfully engaged by the tale of misfortune, of honest merit in distress—it was always new to her, an appealing and personal concern. Tears were in her eyes, a beautiful lament in her voice, as she listened to the tale, and exclaimed, and spoke fervent words of sympathy and comfort. Her heart was reached, her faith never knew misgiving. Something could be done on the spot, food and clothing and money at least were at hand; it was utterly beyond her to weigh and calculate, to defer, to take an impersonal view. I easily see her as she moves to the kitchen window, just outside the door, and calls to the cook within; and Mrs. Chapman appears, small and stout and rosy, not without a look of guarded disapproval in her black eyes—for she too is ready with her resentment at the way our grandmother's charity is " took advantage of." But there it is— it cannot be helped; the stranger is fed, tended, comforted, and departs with something solid in his pocket. Our grandmother had nothing in hers, perhaps; but she dipped into that of Mrs. Chapman —whose weekly " book," it used to be said, was largely filled with these irregular entries. " Poor man (one eye), two-and-six; poor man (wooden leg), five shillings; poor woman (two babies), ten shillings "—such would be the record of very much of the housekeeping at Earlham.

Let us believe that there were many more grateful and encouraged spirits, at the end of it all, than there were confirmed impostors and wastrels. The

24

great glow of devoted affection that our grandmother created around her, during half a century at
Earlham, was a gift to life that cannot be measured.
But there *were* impostors in plenty; they readily
trod the road to Earlham; and if ever one of them
was detected and unmasked, our grandmother's
sorrowful surprise and consternation were intense.
The poor man with the wooden leg, out of work
through no fault of his own, with his children half-
starving, had turned out to be—to be *naughty*, she
would say; " that *naughty* man " was her severest
phrase; her heaviest condemnation was her
wounded tenderness and disappointment. I
suppose she was often disappointed; but each time
seemed a strange lamentable exception, something
that could not happen again. It was forgotten in
what was surely much commoner, a friendship in
which her pure and tender faith was the most help-
ful part of her charitable gift.

There were nooks and corners in the house where
she loved to secrete small stores of good food,
gathered from the dinner-table—grapes, a jelly, a
dumpling, saved for a particular destination.
There was a cupboard of her own, in the hall, with
baskets on a shelf, and in the baskets a basin of
soup or a peach. No one ever saw her drive out
in the afternoon without watching the bestowal
of these under the seats of the carriage, before she
was ready to start; the butler, following her down
the steps with the rug over his arm, had always a
covered basket in his hand. And night after night,
towards bed-time, she was to be seen busy about
her cupboard, with a half-surreptitious air—but

every one knew that she was preparing the meal she always left in the porch for the policeman, for him to find when he made his round at dead of night; and in the silence of the small hours you might hear a window thrown open, and her clear voice calling to him, and an exchange of cheerful christian words.

7

But I forgot—the children were racing to the top of the house, I think, bent on a certain errand. At the very top of the house is a short passage, approached (in the lavish old way) by a staircase at either end, where you reach the attics in the roof. One of these rooms it is that we make for, at any hour of the day; and with my hand once more upon the latch I could hesitate and draw back, before opening the door to such a surge of associations. But who ever hesitated at that door? We tumble in, at all hours; and I believe there is not an inch of it, walls and floor, that I could not exactly describe at this moment.

It is a very bright and pleasant room, with two southern dormer-windows that command the great lawn. A bed is immediately in front of you, as you enter; at the foot of it a narrow sofa; between one of the windows and the fire-place a high-backed arm-chair, with a small round table before it. And in the chair there sits, waiting for you, always quietly ready and pleased at your approach, an old lady, a charmingly dressed and capped and shawled old lady, with soft cheeks, bright eyes, and smooth creamy-white hair under her cap—the old friend, the old nurse, of all our grandmother's many children.

Within *our* memory, that of the children of the children, she had always sat up there in her room; infirmity held her fast. Her eyes met us with a welcome as we entered, with soft clear looks of pleasure, and we huddled round her with the news of the day. Gentle and motherly she was, comfortable to a child; that is the impression that comes back to me from the beginning. It was happy and satisfying to be with her; things went well, the world was secure and friendly in her room. The hours we spent there were hours that could be relied on, unfailingly good and right. How was that? We clustered about her, settled upon her, installed ourselves at her table with our books or paint-boxes; we examined her possessions, we felt at home. And yet, as I look into her soft dimpled face and hear her kind voice, she seems to be using no arts, to be doing nothing to keep the children amused and happy; she simply sits with a light of pleasure on her face, and the children are always good and occupied and entertained in her presence.

And certainly it was not only the children— she was sought out by everybody in the house; her room was a gathering-place for all. Old and young needed her alike; they brought her their news, their troubles, hopes, interests, confiding everything to her deep heart. She sat there all day long in her corner, never leaving her room, and the life around her, age or youth, came to her perpetually for help. She had a gift for all; and though I speak with not

27

much more than the remembrance of her gift for a child, I can easily see that at any age, in all circumstances, one would inevitably turn to her. And still I wonder what it was, the secret she possessed; for even while it is plain that one would go straight to her with the burden of the moment, whatever it might be, her loving wisdom seems to ease it with scarcely a word, with no very vocal sympathy or counsel. But so it was; quietly listening and watching, with just her affection and her simple time-mellowed sagacity, she entered the lives about her, and helped them.

To the children, as I say, it was a sense of well-being, of general rightness, that encompassed them as they sat by her, poring over old treasures and relics that she would produce—or as they wandered and tacked about the room, fingering the hundred small objects with which it was strewn. Every one who came to see her, the children not least, contributed to the thick orderly sprinkling of picture-frames, china ornaments, candlesticks, odds and ends, that covered the walls and shelves—a queer museum, with a personal history to every object. To this day the children could give a fair account of that collection; piece by piece they turned it over, as it steadily grew and grew; there was a name and an occasion attached to everything, perhaps an anecdote. But there was not much story-telling—I am surprised to notice how little. I should have expected to find that we were always clamouring for tales of the past and hanging upon her reminiscences. But that was not her way; she seemed to look on and smile her benediction while we amused ourselves, and the hour prospered under her mere look.

She saw from her window the smooth expanse of the lawn—the lawn that was so great a part of the character of the garden. It was very large, wider than the whole southern front of the house; and some twenty or thirty yards from the garden-door it suddenly shelved up in a steep bank, and the main expanse was on the higher level. It was thus like a raised plain, outspread before the upper windows of the house; to right and left were shrubberies of oak, larch, flowering trees, and beyond it was the sunk fence and the oaks of the park. There was room for widely scattered groups of people, intent here and there on their different games, croquet-hoops on one side, a lawn-tennis net on the other. Shadows lay across it in lengthening jags and promontories through the afternoon; and our old friend, at her high window, watched the light dresses and flannels that twinkled in the distance, in the light and shade. Serenely patient, expecting nothing, demanding nothing, she lived up there, with not a thought or an interest in the world, I suppose, outside the lives of all of us. And presently she heard our feet on the stairs—the children, it might be, or our uncles from their game, or a visiting cousin, or our grandmother, mounting to that high room for brief repose in the midst of her incessant movement and occupation; and the gentle old face by the window lit up for us all, and wrought its spell of harmony and comfort.

Her room was really, I think, the centre of the house, while she lived. There, in all the coming

and going, in the middle of changing life, the
children growing up, the young people marrying,
the new children appearing—in the midst of the
continual stir of hospitality with which Earlham
never ceased to echo, gathering in one generation
after another—there, for so many years, she remained immobile, always the same, always to be
found in her corner. Through the adventures and
possibilities of the day, innumerable they seemed
to us, the thought of climbing her stairs and paying
her a visit ran as an unbroken thread; there was
never an hour when *that* plan was doubtful or
impossible. And for every one else it was the same;
there was one certainty of daily life, to sit by her
side in the window-nook and to tell her what had
happened since yesterday, since this morning.

Far back, in an earlier generation, it was a
tradition of the place, we used to be told, that the
family circle should be drawn together at certain
hours of the day—gathered round a table under a
lamp, perhaps, with books and appropriate occupations, or for talk, seriously directed and regulated—
for a " settlement," anyhow, that being the family
word for it; but it was a tradition that was not at
all in the line of our grandmother's restless active
original genius. She was incapable of living by
fixed plans, stated hours, humdrum habits; and
it comes back to me that the Earlham day reflected
her free spirit. It is impossible to imagine her
leading a settlement. In the whole house she had
not a place of her own, not a sitting-room for her
private use (at least she never used it), not a chair
or a corner sacred to her; she ranged freely, sat for

a moment to scribble a note, threw open a window (that, always), and passed on. It meant that at any time there was no saying where she might be or might not; and the manner of her genius pervaded the house. I remember how a child would feel that there might be important events proceeding and companies assembled somewhere in the house, but that you could not tell where; to fix yourself in one room might always entail your missing an interesting occasion in another. There was very little routine, no centre of gravity in the place—none, that is to say, except in that upper chamber where time stood still. You might find every other room in the house deserted (with all the windows open), no nucleus of life anywhere; but up there was fixity, security, a settlement indeed. And so there was a constant tendency in that direction, and life of all ages set habitually towards our beloved old friend.

8

The Green Room, the Chintz Room, the North Room, the Great Room—but there I pause; the Great Room is too strange and singular to pass by. It was enormous; that is to say, it was no bigger than the drawing-room beneath, but it was exactly as big (extending all over it), and for a bed-room, low-ceilinged, with only two or three far-scattered small windows, it made a broad acre of floor. It was undeniably sinister; with the thin light of its small windows and its huge spread, it was like a prison-cell designed for a giant. Sometimes, waking in the darkness, safely in your own bed elsewhere, you might be visited by the thought of the Great Room—how the moonlight would be trickling over the floor there at that moment, how the deathly silence might be broken by a strange low muttering, then a dull thud, and suddenly a scream rang out— but enough; even to one penetrating there in full daylight, hanging upon the housemaids at their work, the Great Room was sufficiently disquieting.

I believe there was indeed some legend of horror told of that room, but I never knew of it till after-times. To our grandmother fear and its fascinations were unknown; she thought such stories silly and ugly, and altogether discountenanced them. She would not have the sweet old place profaned by ugliness, by idle fancies that are worse than idle, that are false and wrong. If Earlham was haunted, it could only be by spirits of the blest—by Aunt Catherine, perhaps, or Uncle Joseph John, revisiting the old rooms with a soft Quakerly benediction. She was pleased with the thought that some touch of a kindly hand unseen might stir the curtain, some mild and gracious sigh of vanished life, affectionately hovering near, be uttered upon the midnight; it was seemly and right, in a place whose children had loved it so tenderly of old. Perhaps such sweet wistful roaming and wandering might be permitted to a loving spirit—who can say? But terrifying and ugly things of the past are mercifully buried and forgotten; no power can live in them to disturb a place like Earlham, glowing in the love of its children.

The Blue Room, the East Room—as I make the round of the house, images start up, not at all terrifying, from every corner. Each of the rooms at Earlham had its little powder-closet, sliced out of itself or scooped in the wall or pushed forward in an excrescence without; and in the closet of the East Room there was a wondrous bath, more like a tank or cistern, inserted there by Uncle Joseph John, it may be, Borrow's old gentleman in the broad hat. He or one of the others of his day must have had the fantastic notion of bathing in water every morning, from head to foot; and so the powder-closet had been fitted with a great black awful leaden tank, under a wooden lid; I would as soon have taken my bath in the well by the back-door, I remember thinking, as have entrusted myself to that black pit. In the ceiling above it there were perforated holes, for a shower-bath; so that our ancestor was not only immersed, but rained upon from overhead—evidently a man of nerve, and of ideas beyond his age. I picture him bringing his friends to view the curiosity. But after him no one apparently, any more than I myself, had the nerve to plunge into his pit. It was never used; only a child would sometimes climb on to the wooden lid and thump out its hollow echo, or tug it open a few inches and peer into the empty black depth with a shudder.

The East Room, with its broad windows looking to the green back-yard, brings me to the end of the chief passage, near our nursery; the East Room door and the nursery door (one of the five) are left and right towards the end of the passage. One drifts back into the bright bare nursery. From thence you can pass from room to room, the whole length of the house, without touching the passage at all. Every room opens into the next; there is our grandmother's charming panelled bed-room, with the old portrait of the unknown lady in blue, framed in the woodwork of the chimney-piece; there is another room and another (our grandmother's sitting-room, where she seldom happens to sit); there is a scrap of a dressing-room, and then there is the Ante-room Chamber, the nicest room in the house, assigned to the principal guest of the moment. That was a delightful room—with windows on two sides, a vast four-poster, and a door in one corner where you fell down a little private stair-case in the wall, and were shed into the great dim ante-room, of which I have spoken already. And this was the corner of the house where Aunt Catherine, if any-where, should come straying out of the past, roam-ing among her memories in the silence of the night, and just betraying herself sometimes, perhaps, by a light sigh or murmur of full-hearted tenderness, as she treads the well-known stairs again. The Ante-room Chamber was her room, during the long life-time that she spent at Earlham.

She was our great-grandfather's sister, and Elizabeth Fry's and Uncle Joseph John's; there were many more of them too, a large gay party, and Catherine was the eldest. Their father brought them to make their home at Earlham, long ago; and their beautiful mother (exquisite she is, in a picture by Gainsborough) died when the eldest was still very young. There were eleven of them, a blooming brood, and Catherine ruled the house. She lived on and on, continually at Earlham, when the rest of them scattered off into the world; she lived with her brother and his wife. Our grandmother, as a girl and in the time of her first marriage (to a nephew of Aunt Catherine's), had known and gratefully loved her. When she spoke of " dear Aunt Catherine," it gave us a sense of reaching back into the dawn of time. That our grandmother, a girl, had known such antiquities, called them Uncles and Aunts—nothing could be more legendary than that.

9

These old Gurneys were people of note, in their degree; together they made a group that is still expressive and marked with character. They were handsome, gifted, humane; and as they grew and reached their moral stature they might fairly be called very good. Their saintliness bequeathed a savour to the place; but their lighter youth left a ringing echo that had never died out. Is it supposed that a family of young Friends, four or five generations ago, were of necessity bred and trained in puritanical strictness, their merry-making frowned upon, their chatter silenced with pious admonition? Look, then, at the seven Miss Gurneys, all blooming and sparkling, well known over the country-side in their scarlet cloaks or habits; there was no unnatural solemnity in that bright chorus. Once, we were told, they all joined hands across the Norwich road and stopped the mail-coach—a gay-coloured picture, under a frosty winter sky.

Their father, I should think, was a worthy and

35

not an interesting man. All his history is that he married the charming Gainsborough lady, Catherine Bell was her name, and that his affairs prospered far enough to enable him to plant his family at Earlham in 1786—two good achievements in a life not otherwise notable. No legend ever grew about his name; he seems to have sat in the background placidly till he died. His children were of a very different stamp. Even when they left off their scarlet cloaks and purple boots and took to stricter ways, clothing themselves in drab and dun, their originality was never quenched. They had the secret of giving a kind of lilt or fling to their pious exercises, or some of them had at any rate, and in their saintly old age they were never quite cut off from their merry youth. They created legend wherever they went; bits of it that clung to various corners of the house and garden at Earlham were familiar to the children in a later day. Here, in the Ante-room Chamber, was where good Catherine used to collect her small sisters round her (the very type and pattern of a settlement) and encourage their young ideas, sympathetically eliciting and directing them. She managed her big family (beginning to do so when she was herself about seventeen) with tender tact and judgment; and she had the satisfaction of sitting nearly all her life long at Earlham to watch their virtue and felicity in their different careers.

Often I have tried to picture that party; and I get flashes of sight of them that are strangely familiar. But that is in the garden, mostly, where I have not yet arrived; and the vision that faces

me now, in the doorway of Aunt Catherine's room,
belongs to our own day, when all those old Friends,
though they lived long, were many years dead and
gone. But in truth the figure that I see stepping
forth with splendid dignity and grace, with a grand
air, sweeping her skirt regally about her, might
seem to have emerged from old Catherine's time,
though from a greater world than hers ever was.
This striking and wonderful lady—whom it so
happens that I catch sight of, framed in the doorway
that leads to our grandmother's sitting-room—
treads the homely floor as though it were the gallery
of a palace, with a shining parquet stretching a
hundred yards before her. She advances like an
ambassadress, like a Grand Duchess—she moves
historically, bringing something august into the
place and the occasion. Her head should have been
tired and plumed; but she needed no plumes—
they seemed to sweep the lintel, whatever she wore.
She was old, as I remember her, grey-haired, her
face nobly marked with age; but her figure was
slender and upright, there was youth in her flowing
movement. I have seen no one to match her, to
approach her, for perfect and natural grandeur—it
is the only word.

She was the daughter of one of the old Friends of
whom I have been speaking, Samuel by name, and
she inherited all the free originality and charm
which they had to bequeath. But she had added
much more that was entirely her own; and what
it was that she had added I measure by looking at
the home of her birth—very vividly known to me
by legend, though it had long vanished at the time

of *our* appearance. In one of those plain and opulent suburban mansions, round which and over which the tide of East London has flowed in the last half-century—one of those sound big Georgian villas, with plenty of well-kept flower-beds and shrubberies and hot-houses, where solid and expensive comfort was joined with a dread of worldly show, where the spirit of an early Christian was engaged in large financial interests and operations— that was where she had been bred, with her brothers and sisters. It was a closely compacted world; and as it exists, or something like it, in certain well-known pages—Sophia Alethea Newcome lived in such a house, and so did the parents of Ruskin—it strikes the imagination oppressively, no doubt. But I like to think that in this world the Society of Friends brought a brisker infusion; they were lighter, they were less solemn than Sophia Alethea, with her tracts and her droning preachers; they wore their piety more easily, more genially, less as a burden and a bondage. Did they not? At any rate our good great-grandfather, Samuel Gurney, was a man of wise and sunny humour. He carried up to London, from Earlham, some strain of whimsical humanity that he never lost, a shrewd appreciative chuckle; I speak as though I had seen and heard it, for I *did* see and hear it, transmitted to certain of his family. And so his household, solid as it was, could never be heavy; there could be nothing like a drone or a dull sing-song in his piety.

But that Quaker-world, nevertheless, was aloof and aloft and detached from the general structure of life; it strikes one as held in suspense, with space all round it, nowhere rooted in the soil. Consider, for instance, the old family-circle at Earlham. If you had fallen in upon them on a summer afternoon, a century ago and more, when they were chattering and roaming about the place, or grouped about the garden, reading, drawing, stitching, it would have seemed a perfect picture of an English country-home, the beautiful old house and park with its bevy of fresh young daughters among the ancestral oaks; nothing could look more natural, traditional, after the home-grown fashion, in the line of English ways. But it was not so, really. I don't only mean that these people were new-comers, the daughters of a prosperous merchant who had worked his way up to the ripe style and dignity of Earlham—who had not ripened *with* it. They were new-comers; but there would be nothing against the English tradition in that, after all; not once or twice in our story have new men rooted themselves upon old acres. That, however, was exactly what these people did not do; they came, they brought a blessing, but they never—how shall I put it?—they never involved or implicated themselves with the earth they trod. In all their long tenure of Earlham, extending over three generations, they never owned the soil upon which it stood; and though the fact may have meant nothing, or nothing more than a chapter of accidents, still it seems in a way symbolical. The Quaker-circle was a law to itself; it had its own idiom, not of language only.

They did not belong to the country-side, they did not belong to the world. Their Christian piety took them on Sundays, not to the ivy-tangled flint

39

church at their gates, where the ancient threads of village life were gathered up, but to some blank meeting-house in a chance back-street of Norwich. Their faith, their fervour, their charitable hearts were wide and deep; but around them was the void, isolating them in a world of their own. I am evidently trying to say that they were primitive Christians. And when they went out and became missionaries and reformers, like Aunt Fry among the prisoners, touring the capitals of Europe, reasoning graciously with kings and statesmen— then more than ever they were distinguished from the world, they were unlike other people, they were Friends. When they went out and became bankers and merchants, and prospered exceedingly, it was doubtless the same—at least I hope it was; their prosperity, we always understood and believed, was founded upon the rigidest Friendly principles.

I conclude, then, that Samuel Gurney's solid establishment to the east of London—the place still exists as an open playground, somewhere in the brick waste of the Stratford region—was delightful, cheerful, hospitable, generous; but unrelated, unconditioned, in the widest sense unworldly. I see no background to it, nothing to link it with history. And yet there steps out this daughter of the house, this noble great lady with her imperial tread, who crosses the room as though it were the *galerie des glaces*, and she herself serenely, unconsciously at home there.

She indeed had issued forth from the close circle and had joined the march of the world; and when I recall her bountiful and vivacious kindness to the

40

children of our generation, to us, an air of the *grand siècle* seems to breathe through it, an initiation for the children into the meaning of style. But to follow my memories of this wondrous great-aunt would take me too far; this is only a glimpse that I chance to get of her at Earlham. And there is another fleeting picture—in the same room, our grandmother's sitting-room—that I may place beside it, for it is a picture of another member of old Samuel's large family. One of our great-uncles, this, and a very fine old gentleman, though not magnificent and European, like his sister; he was British and jolly, with a lovely wink of slyness and mystery when he drew his hand from his pocket and held it out, the broad palm studded with shillings and half-crowns, for us to choose the coin we preferred. He was stone-deaf, and it needed a great deal of resolution to pipe one's thanks into the gaping mouth of his bright trumpet. But at this moment, in the sitting-room, what was it that had gone wrong? Nothing serious, nothing to matter, only enough to ruffle his genial face with just a passing, pouting breeze of displeasure—enough to make him present his trumpet at his daughter, bending over him, with an indignant and question-ing flourish. What had she to say about it? Nothing except that she was so sorry, so very sorry—but her pretty voice rose higher and higher, wailing into the trumpet-mouth. "I'm so-o-o-o sorry"; and the breeze passed, geniality shone back—and it is all vanished and gone, leaving only the little unefface-able memory of the fresh-coloured old gentleman, with pursed mouth and inquiring eye, his daughter stooping over his chair, and the clear soaring wail of her distress. Who shall say what a child will remember and what forget?

10

The sitting-room gave you an impression of big high windows, a matted floor, some rather spindly gilt furniture—but especially, perhaps, of a quantity of water-colour pictures, evidently all by one hand, with which the walls were covered. They were all pictures of Earlham, the house, the park, the village; there may have been twenty or thirty of them. They were lightly tinted old things, done with a good deal of accomplishment; and resolutely picturesque, as though the drawing-master had stood looking over the shoulder of the artist, pointing out that the bough of a tree should always chance to arch over the foreground, and a figure in a red cloak pass across the middle distance in a woodland scene. The facts of the landscape gave way if they conflicted with the rules of the game, which the artist played conscientiously; but they were pretty pictures, not without an elegant distinction, and on the whole they were faithful portraits of the place.

The artist was Richenda Gurney, sister of old Samuel, and one of the blooming seven in red coats who stopped the coach. She was very fluent with brush and pencil, covered many walls with her framed pictures, and filled a pile of sketch-books with drawings of mossy cottages and ivied ruins wherever she went. She married a clergyman, a real Established rector, Mr. Cunningham of Lowes-

toft church; and then she left being a Quakeress,
and " went over "—I dare say it was not far to go.
Mr. Cunningham's church services, I have heard,
were very comfortable and homely. On Sunday
evenings especially, when the lamps burnt bright
and warm in the church, and the parishioners came
trooping into their seats, and the sea-wind moaned
without—then was the time for Aunt Cunningham
to enjoy herself among her flock. Evening church
was infinitely grateful and satisfying to them all—
a cheerful, sociable scene, with the bright lamp-light
falling on all the well-known faces, rosy in the
pleasant warmth after a cold walk. They rise from
their knees, Aunt Cunningham and her friends, and
settle themselves in their places with beaming looks,
disposing their preparations about them, their wraps
and Bibles and hymn-books, for an hour that is the
treat of the whole week. " Here we all are again,"
they seem to say, radiantly glancing. " Now! "—
and off they go in a fine florid hymn-tune, " Helms-
ley " I hope, with plenty of trailing sweeps up to
high notes, in which enjoyment can really give
tongue.

It is seventy, eighty, ninety years ago; but I
could imagine I had seen it. Uncle and Aunt
Cunningham were greatly honoured and cherished
in the legend as it reached us; and the legend had a
particular association with Earlham in the coming
time, the time that eventually brought the children
thither of whom I speak. There was a curate at
Lowestoft, fresh from Cambridge—a tall, lean
young man, with a large brow and a narrow pointed
chin, looking like a scholar and a student. Before

long he married and came to live at Earlham; he was our grandfather—to be accurate, our *step*-grandfather, as I have said.

Earlham, it will be understood, had first been the home of the big Quaker family, the eleven brothers and sisters; and then, when they scattered, of one of the brothers, Joseph John. He died in the forties; and what was then to become of Earlham, which had made itself so beloved to half a century of Gurneys? The question was asked by a Gurney of the next generation, John by name, who was living with his young wife in a house down by the church, in Earlham village. They walked up to the Hall, the day after old Joseph John had been buried, walked round the garden and on to the great lawn, and looked up at the empty windows of the house. Who will live here now?—is there nobody to carry on the good tradition? They asked and wondered, and they might have wished to do so themselves; it seemed beyond them at the time. The house stood empty for a few years, but only for a few; then this John Gurney of the new generation, son of old Samuel, brought his young wife and their small children to live there after all. For himself it was not a long sojourn; he died very soon. But his young widow, still very young, lived there for nearly fifty years, till the end of her days, and she was our grandmother.

So young, so pretty, so good, with her family of small children, she was much befriended in her widowhood by the surviving old Gurneys—who indeed had known and loved her, I suppose, from the beginning, for the home of her parents was near by,

44

in the Cathedral Close of Norwich, and from there she had been married. And now she was alone at Earlham, and many of the old Gurneys were dead and gone by this time, but there were still a few of them left. Catherine was gone, the eldest of the eleven; she had been the best friend of all, and she had lived just long enough to give her blessing to a new Catherine Gurney, our grandmother's one daughter. Of those that remained of the old generation, the kindest and best-beloved, no doubt, was Aunt Cunningham at Lowestoft. The cheerful rectory by the sea was well-known to our grandmother's children, and she herself would be made thrice-welcome there.

And so in process of time she married again, and Earlham received the tall thin benevolent stranger, and a new tradition was begun there that was no break with the old. The new master of the house was now the rector of St. Giles's, the big church with the fine old tower and belfry on the outskirt (then and long after the outskirt) of Norwich, as you leave the city by the Earlham road. He was rector there for thirty years, and I know something of the many great works that he achieved in the place, he and our grandmother together. But I speak only of what I can *see*, by my own memory or that of others, and here sight fails me; for in our day, as I have mentioned, his cure was that of the red-tiled cottages at Earlham and Colney. I only see exactly how his tall black figure would disappear across the lawn, trudging steadily, as he set off by the fields for the Norwich road; and I guess that his name is not forgotten in the parish of St. Giles—William

45

Nottidge Ripley, a memorable rector there for
thirty years.

II

The new tradition at Earlham was very like the
old; but in certain ways it was a much better one.
Our grandparents struck deeply into the soil of the
life around them; that sense of a space-encircled,
insulated household, which I got from the older
story of the place, could not survive for a day in the
new condition of things which they created. Earlham was no longer only a family affair, the centre
of a close circle; it was diffused, spreading year by
year in widest commonalty. Our grandfather, though
he believed that he believed in a doctrine both narrow
and harsh—how narrow, how blackly intolerant was
revealed when it appeared in others of a different
clay—lived upon free spiritual emotions that broadened continually, I judge, as he advanced to old
age. And as for our grandmother, her unfettered,
untutored, impulsive heart made nothing of any
barriers; it ignored distinctions and conventions, it
ranged where it would, swiftly responding to any
human call.

She was one who acted always on impulse, on
the beat of the moment; and since she never knew
a thought that was in sight of being a selfish one,
the whole surface of her life was sensitive and quick
to the world about her. A heart like hers can live
without scheme or plan, and yet live in perfect
and consistent harmony with itself; for behind all
its wayward expression there can never be but a
single motive. Whatever she said or did was

46

whatever seemed desirable and inevitable then and there, on the instant; but it was only the form, the manner, that was unexpected, surprising, sometimes even disconcerting. It was prompted by the pure flame of rapture, I can call it nothing else, which was her constant inspiration—an ardour of faith and love that was both serenely deep, and also to the end, for all her many sorrows, inextinguishably gay.

She had great dignity, the kind of native dignity and distinction that never needs to take or dreams of taking a single thought for itself. Matronly and motherly, with a fine bearing and sweep of soft raiment, she met the guest and presided over the lavish hospitality of Earlham. And yet it seems to me, looking back, that she was never quite in the place or sustaining the position that you would expect. She has just for the moment slipped out of her place—has given up her seat in the carriage, say, to some tired woman she has sighted on the road, while she herself walks home—or she has disappeared up into the gallery in church to direct the organist (it was really a harmonium) or help a mother embarrassed with a restless child—or she is missed at the head of the table and found at her cupboard in the hall, secreting something that she has filched from one of the dishes for a sick friend; and always with an air of explaining that she is really not doing what she clearly is, that she has *not* left her place, that she will be back there so soon that it doesn't count. Then she would join the laugh against herself, but never quite admit that it was justified; there was always a special reason for the aberration of the moment that explained it quite away. In her last years, when she was supposed to rest late and not to appear at morning prayers, there would be heard a light rustle on the staircase, while our grandfather was reading and expounding—a rustle, a faint sigh, as she sat by the banisters, believing herself out of sight; and well I see her afterwards when she protests, still seated on the stairs, that indeed she has practically stayed in bed.

Best of all, perhaps, I see her as she was so often to be seen, in the garden of an early summer morning—very early, before the white dew on the lawn has been touched by any footstep and while everything still sparkles and twinkles, " herrlich wie am ersten Tag." To the garden in the freshness of its magic she would often be drawn; at any hour she might be descried, lightly, informally gowned and wrapped, pacing the gravel-paths with her easy gracious upright movement. One may have seen many people enjoying the charm and benediction of nature and drinking in the purity of the morning with delight; but I am sure I never saw any one who rejoiced in the hour like our grandmother. She moved through the garden, she trod the walks, uplifted and transfigured, as though with triumph and exultation in the loveliness that surrounded her. When the first sunshine shot across the blue-shadowed grass you might discern her, looking from your window, as she strayed along the path that bounded the lawn, on the further side of it from the house, separated only by the sunk fence from the great old oaks of the park. Slowly she moved, her white and trailing garments gathered round her, her eyes gazing widely, her face alight with praise and joy. New every morning was her rapture in the gift of the world's beauty; the wonder never grew less, no sorrow dimmed or defeated it. And mixed with her joy in the moment there was always the inner thought of the celestial beauty, unimaginably beyond this earthly, rarer even than this which seemed already beautiful beyond conception. And so as she passed and re-passed she carried with her a very radiance of adoration, magnifying the work of her maker and giving thanks for ever.

12

The traditions of her birth and training were very inconsistent in one respect. The natural beauty of the world might belong to the kingdom of heaven, for it was the work of the great artificer and glorified his power; the spirit of religion breathed in the divine freshness of the morning, green and blue and gold; holiness was there manifest, and to lose your-self in contemplation of the marvel could only lead you higher. But beauty of man's creation, the work of the created, lay under a suspicion; it must justify itself, the presumption was against its purity and sanctity unless it was explicit in its lofty pur-pose. It is an old story; I cannot but think that the monkish distrust of beauty in any form, the beauty of field and wood like any other, not ex-pressly dedicated to the service of the most high, is a more reasonable perversity. Let it all be disgrace-ful together, everything that enchants the eye or the ear or the imagination—why not? But still, if you are very certain of the badness and blackness of man's heart, I suppose you must assume that the work of his hands is tainted, unless it bears a recognized phylactery; and you may believe in the innocence of a bird or a flower, that no man made, even though it is beautiful. Only man is vile—that is your logic.

But if you intensely and affectionately believe in the goodness of man's heart, in the rightness of his intention—and yet the old mistrustful tradition holds you, bidding you beware, setting you on your guard in the presence of the unsanctioned fervour of an artist: is not this a perverse confusion to have drifted into? I return again and again to a sense of resentment, not indeed personal, that people like our grandparents should have been impelled to assure themselves, or to feel that they ought to be assured, of something dubious, deceitful, not to be trusted, lurking generally within the soul of art. No false doctrine, it is true, can greatly matter in the lives of such people; because their own true nature, so much larger than the teaching imposed upon it, has its way of flouting perversity in any form. But something remains, something that checks and crosses the natural impulse of a spirit ardently eager and awake. The imagination, crying out for nourishment, is neglected, discouraged; one's private world does not get its due enlargement.

Our grandmother's quick and sympathetic fancy, I see, was never finally disheartened by such treatment. It was always ready to seize a chance and to carry her beyond the circle of ideas and emotions of which she traditionally approved. Remembering the recurring scene that took place when she found herself drawn into the reading of a book, a secular story-book, I understand how her genius must have been straining towards its own. Small its chances were, but it clutched them. Secular books were never conspicuous at Earlham; they tended to hide in our uncles' rooms, to turn their faces to the wall, to be wrapped in non-committal covers of paper; it was not at all a house where the " last novel " would lightly lie on the table. But now and then, perhaps, one of them would happen to fall in the way of the mistress of the house; she might take it up to glance at a page, half-protesting; and then the sequel was certain and well-known. She was absorbed, she was lost; late as it might be, she would run through the story and finish it to the end before she slept. She was an active, swift-glancing reader, when she read; she had a hand and eye that seemed pre-disposed to a book, like the skill of a craftsman born. She turned the page with none of the cautious or painful circumspection of those who do not habitually live with books, who read as though they were conscientiously verifying a doubtful statement. She was lost until she had finished the book; and her children knew well the gush of indignation in her voice, next morning, when her self-reproach, the thought of precious wasted hours, turned to rend the poor book and its author—such a silly, foolish book, worse than foolish, snaring one to waste time upon idle trifles. Small indications— but they showed how an imagination, diligently discountenanced, would still live on and watch for its opportunity and make the most of it; with that

51

old tradition, the invention of souls successfully chilled and dulled, always at hand to afflict a tender conscience and extort its payment.

It is a familiar story indeed; no doubt there have always been opulent natures misfitted by the beliefs and opinions of smaller folk. Beliefs that had arisen in hearts that to hers were as the crab-apple to the golden apricot—ideas that could no more have sprung in the climate of her life than dead-sea fruit in a green pasture—these were somehow to be kept and held as though they were prompted by inner voices, as though they expressed one's deepest need. Somehow the adjustment was to be made, and so made that one should never even notice the discrepancy oneself; the submissive heart must accept these unlikely intruders and be convinced that they are its very offspring. And as for being so convinced, it would seem that there is no difficulty in that; never for a moment could such a spirit as this of which I am thinking be inclined to contradict, to question, to disown the notions so foisted upon it. Theoretically you are limited to a very narrow path, and it is woe to those without; theoretically your scheme of faith is closely bound about, and its edges are terribly decided. But after all it is to be seen that nothing on earth will really constrain you, will be allowed to dictate to such a spirit as this; charity, warm and ripe, instantly oblivious of the precepts it has accepted, soars above them and escapes. *Anima naturaliter christiana*—it is not to hold or to bind by jealous and timorous devices. The most that these can effect is now and then to distress the Christian conscience with a needless, unmerited

52

pang. It is the triumph of the meaner souls—not a great one, when all is said.

13

Her name before she married was Laura Pearse. She was one of several sisters, and they were the daughters of an old gentleman whose legend had long fallen dim in our time; he must have been dead for many years. Some hint in an anecdote or two, some glimpse of a mild old clergyman sitting drowsily acquiescent, in the simplicity of extreme age, is connected with the impression of the drawing-room at Earlham on a summer afternoon—it was great-grandfather Pearse who sat there, and I vaguely see him, though I can never have seen him with my own eyes. In his last years, it may be, his mind and memory gently failed him a little; I think he had already lost his remarkable wife, and he might come to Earlham on a long visit to his daughter. Nodding in his chair in the drawing-room, through a hot afternoon, he would forget the hours, and might almost, one would suppose, be himself forgotten. But there was some young member of the family told off, I gather, to keep him company; he wants no talk or entertainment, but a young granddaughter can sit with her sewing in the window-seat, as quiet as a mouse, and be ready to read to him, to run errands for him, if he should rouse himself to need her. So there she sits, and I well understand that as the sun blazes outside and the wood-pigeons croon in the oaks by the west lawn, and in the room the hush grows deeper, the old man placidly reposing, the hours are long and

53

restless for the girl over her petticoat-hem in the window. She would have an inkling that our beloved grandmother, in her filial piety, would welcome her aged father, tend him and care for him, be the truest of daughters—but would not, could not possibly, sit serenely stitching in a corner through an endless afternoon, while her father dreamed and drowsed in the stillness. So much as that her activity could not endure; the young girl must charge herself with that particular duty; and I think the young girl, the picture of obedience, will be clear in her own mind that her elders have shifted a task upon her that none of them are eager to undertake.

Well, it so happened that outside the window where she sat there grew an old greengage-tree, trained against the wall; and on one of these long afternoons she discovered that there were green-gages, bursting ripe, within her reach. She solaced her vigil—and so, as you easily see, the hour took its little niche in her memory and was there, years afterwards, to be brought out and told as a story, in thrilling detail, to a child. By means of those juicy sun-cracked greengages a vision of great-grandfather Pearse was transmitted; and of all that he said and did and was in the world, for the better part of a century, perhaps that single somnolent hour of his life will be the last to perish entirely.

He had had a very remarkable wife; and as for his daughters, the picture that they make, issuing in their girlhood from their modest and secluded corner of the world, is one that always strikes me with new surprise. A plain little establishment in

54

the Cathedral Close of Norwich, afterwards trans-
ferred to a village-rectory far out in the country,
an inaccessible mud-bound village near the Norfolk
coast—and a simple old rector, with a wife and a
family of daughters: you see the picture at once, it
is as familiar as daisies on the green. The good
father of the flock, the mother bustling about
among the cottage-wives, the rosy-cheeked daughters trudging the lanes in their stout boots—all
these you know by heart, you cannot mistake them.
And scarcely a point in this picture, as it instantly
forms itself, is correct; the household of great-
grandfather Pearse, at Martham Rectory three
generations ago, was different and odd and rare—
and I wonder whether it seemed as inexplicable in
its time as it does to me now, in the light of these
days.

Pretty, fantastic, paradoxical, it seems to me
now; but perhaps it did not then affect a beholder
as unlikely. It was not so very strange, perhaps,
that the parson's wife in a lonely inaccessible village
—most inaccessible, even now—should be the kind
of person our great-grandmother was. She might
have been a stirring woman in the parish, one who
directed her household with energy, active in
kitchen and dairy, setting her maids to the spinning-
wheel, gossiping with a crony or so in the village,
perhaps at feud with the farmer's wife, perhaps
nourishing ambitions for her daughters and culti-
vating relations with the local gentry. It would
have been a thankless field, I must think, for energy
and ambition; and I should imagine her a little
toughened and roughened by the struggle, a little

chafed by the inevitable limitations of her scope. What could she do in such a desert? How could she bend the age-long immobility of her surroundings to her busy will? Above all, what could she do in her small circumstances with a troop of daughters, however blooming? A losing, losing struggle, surely, in which her defeated spirit would be worn down, keeping only enough of its sharpness to be irritated by her husband's contented acquiescence in obscurity and poverty and monotony. On these lines the picture fills itself with abundance of detail.

She sat, as a matter of fact, in her small drawing-room, exquisite and elegant, daintily toying with some scrap of cobweb needlework—she reclined upon a spindle-legged couch, far aloof from the stir and gossip of the vulgar. She smiled very kindly upon her parish, but graciously, distantly; when she stepped forth, on occasion, passed down the lane and entered some humble village-parlour— swept and prepared for her visit, be very sure— she was like one who confers a charming favour, and so she was received. Her demeanour, no doubt, represented the natural tribute to her position and to that of her rustic friends; on both sides it was understood, I take it. Such was the right mutual attitude of refinement and rusticity, each good of its kind, each injured by any attempt to interfere with the appointed order of things. Respect on both sides, familiarity on neither, was her rule; and it is not so much the validity of the rule that one may question—it may be a very good one—as the mere fact that in that far seclusion it should be possible to hold to it so consistently. There is a magnificence beyond all probability—here is my paradox—in that power to shoulder the responsibility of high manners all alone and unaided, with nobody to see the effect, nobody to join you in keeping the standard at that high level, nobody to notice if you let it sink. This little great-grandmother carried out the tradition she knew as easily, to all appearance, in her lonely parsonage as she might have maintained it before the eyes and with the support of the world. Perhaps I exaggerate the difficulty; but when I think of her rising, day after day, to the sight of the same old church-tower and the sound of the same farm-waggon upon the road, with nothing else (one may say) to think of till next morning, I can only wonder at the untouched perfection of her elegant style.

So she reclined, toying with her scrap of embroidery and adorned with scrupulous nicety of lace and lawn—a rare little image of the old world. She breathed the air of refinement, perfumed by rose-leaves in blue-and-white jars on a lacquered cabinet. Perhaps after breakfast, delicately equipping herself for the task, she would collect the Chinese tea-cups with fastidious finger-tips and wash them; to that extent a gentlewoman will properly take a share in the work of the house. Otherwise—what does she do? Her social resources are few indeed in those wilds. Her pride, as fine as her porcelain, discriminates sharply, and I dare say her manner towards the doctor's wife, and the farmer's and the schoolmaster's (if there was one), has more than a shade of condescension. On the other hand, imagine her horror at the notion of pursuing a social ambition in higher spheres—of vulgarly pushing one's way with a worldly motive. Besides she is not rich, her movements are strictly limited. On the whole she sits at home; and surely there must be a great deal of unoccupied time upon her hands.

Yes, no doubt; but then she has other resources. She lived in a world of her own, a world of roseate and romantic fancy, a kind of egg-shell fairyland never penetrated by the common prose of things. And moreover she had her talents, and she could use them for an admirable purpose. In her dainty, orderly life she could see from afar the dangers of the outer world and its dread temptations; it was laid upon her to shield and to warn the exposed. A worthy work, she might well think it, to devote her gift to such a cause. And a gift she had; she could write a long and fairly coherent and expressive romance, full of lamentable incident that illustrated the deceitfulness of riches and the doom of frivolity. I think she did not write more than one; but one novel makes a novelist, after all, and a novelist she became, she was, she remained. Earthly Idols, two volumes in pink cloth—it was the story of a dreadfully (but justly) afflicted heroine, who set her heart upon idols of clay, who saw them torn from her one by one, and who perished at last, she herself—with a heart, I hope and think, finally chastened and purified—in a storm at sea. Such at least would seem to have been the motive in the author's imagination, though she undermined it a little by failing to impute, from the beginning, any touch of earthliness to her Rosalie. That heroine had always a spirit so pure that the logic of her inexorable punishment is not clear; the novelist, I suppose, could not bring herself to disparage her lovely Rosalie, and the moral had to suffer. The high purpose is plain, nevertheless; the very profits of the sale (but there may have been none) were dedicated in advance to the enlightenment of the heathen.

I like to think of the authoress, bending gracefully over her manuscript in her tiny drawing-room, her neat little hand moving smoothly over the pages. It is a perfectly urbane and civilized picture, but quite out of place in that rather forlorn setting of Martham village. The outer edges of Norfolk can be dreary, in the barer regions towards the sea. You reach Martham after leaving everything else behind, and only then; it is a cluster of cottages round a straggling green, and the diminutive parsonage stands under the morning shadow of a great square church-tower. A gaunt and dilapidated old pile the church must have been, when Earthly Idols was composed in its shadow; and the village had no picturesque attraction. The sea-wind whines, though the sea is not in sight. As autumn darkened and the mist rose and the mud deepened, it must have seemed a place of far exile, one would say, for a creature so delicately formed and finished. Did she never, on mornings of steely east wind, in long wailing nights of storm, feel a pang of rebellion, reaching out in spirit to the humaner world for which she was so suitably gifted? Instead, she had only her stumping, drawling congregation, immitigably bucolic. Who was there to recognize and appreciate her style?

EARLHAM

There were at least her children and her grand-
children, and she deeply touched their imagination.
She lived on and on in their memory, long after she
was under the turf of the churchyard, as a little fine
model of bearing and adornment, never to be sur-
passed in its kind. Elegance is very attractive to
the young, and they take it most seriously; the
sight of it works powerfully in the stirring and
forming of a small fancy. Our great-grandmother of
the trim thatched parsonage is still the impersonation of gentility for her descendants. Always
perfect in her ways and habits, she looks watchfully,
critically, upon the behaviour of the children round
her and instils her principles of gracious deportment.
They are scarcely those, perhaps, of the thatched
parsonage of to-day; not there would a young
granddaughter now sit over her darning or her
hemming, intent upon dealing with it in business-
like style, and hear the voice of her grandmother in
expostulation, silvery-tinkling—" Not like that,
dear, not so earnestly; you should *play* with it,
dear, *play* with it! "—while she illustrates the right
style of negligent grace with little easy flourishes of
her own needle, lightly hovering over her ornamen-
tal scrap of white gossamer.

14

But that was long ago; it is all legend and tradition. I come back to our own day and to the
hushed and darkened drawing-room at Earlham,
where the blinds are pulled down against the afternoon blaze. There is a light bitter-sweet fragrance
from the phloxes in the strangely mixed bouquet,

60

feathered with asparagus, which stands in the middle of the round table—where the lamp stands in the evening. Long ago the old man of whom I have spoken sat and slumbered here, while the girl hung out of window to reach the greengages on the wall. But the old man is dead, he is a story of the past; and his granddaughter now tells it to a pair of children, small cousins of hers, who beset her with their demands. Tales of her childhood—we wanted more and more of them; but chiefly we wanted the same anecdotes, two or three, over and over again—and in the exact original form, which we could always supply (and still could, I should think, to-day) if our cousin's memory faltered. Our demands followed her everywhere, at all times of day; and when she was " dressing for dinner " it was the best chance of all. Then we were free from interruption. I discern a child who stands by the dressing-table in the tiny Chintz Room, fingering the pin-cushion and the brushes, listening enthralled.

These stories became dramas, brilliantly visual, as our cousin told them. Brushing and plaiting her long rich hair, she picked up the details of the scene, found nobly descriptive words for them, hung thrillingly upon her climax; and when she reached it, with a gesture of her brush or her handful of hair-pins she would act it to the life—the listener throbbed with satisfaction. They were beautiful stories, not so much for their stirring incident as for the sharp actuality of their setting. An incident has no value in itself, it is exactly as interesting as the artist can make it; and this cousin was an artist indeed. Ah, that strange wild comedy of the tapioca pudding—the plate-full of loathsome jellied lumps that had been placed before her, a well-behaved child, and that suddenly, swiftly, she had tilted with one turn of her hand into the napkin upon her lap; she was lunching out, you see, and it was a critical occasion, and she was on her best behaviour; but the strange deed was done in a flash, and *nobody noticed*—it is a fact. She was able to conceal the warm sagging mass, carry it out and bury it in the garden afterwards; and by the time when she reached the burial in the shrubbery emotion had risen and surged and toppled over in a gurgle of the listener's approval—she had told the story just as she had told it before, in its classical form, and on the whole, among many good, it was surely her very best.

The Chintz Room was minute; it just fitted into one of the gables in the oldest part of the house—the gable, curved and scrolled, which carried the date of the battle of Edgehill. It was a tiny room without a fire-place, and the small-paned casement window almost filled one side of it. You craned up and stood on tiptoe to search the cracks and crevices of the window-sill; for there was always a rumour that a beast, a centipede, had once walked out of one of them, straggling on all its feet, to the proper horror of our cousin who occupied the room. It would be a triumph to entice it forth again; but that was not necessary—you had only to cry that you had caught sight of it, just for a moment, and our dear cousin was ready with brilliant shrieks of dismay. It was well worth while to repeat the scare, several times. Or again you could stand by the

table, mounted upon a stool, and turn the pages of
the little fat leather volume, her hymn-book; and
let me state the fact plainly, it was in that volume
that this present author first found a page, a printed
page, turn intelligible to the eye; it seemed to
happen in a minute, after all that useless grind over
spelling-books and such-like at home. I could
read, it appeared; some magic had operated. But
what a beautiful picture of the child, balanced upon
the footstool by the dressing-table, reading "Once in
royal David's city" out aloud, so confidently, so
piously—if it fails to strike another as charming, I
assure you it struck the child. A warm and satis-
factory sense of holiness, the kind of solemn aura
that hangs about the children in a Sunday-book—
could one pretend to be unconscious of this, for all
one's proper meekness? One could only hope that
it was not unobserved; and I dare say indeed that
the brightly glancing young lady, brushing out the
long golden coils of her hair, observed and smiled.

The window of the Chintz Room looked away to
the last of the sunset, and in the long twilight,
fading at last, the tiny chamber grew grey and dim.
It had earned its name, I suppose, in ancestral days;
there was no shine or crackle of chintz there in our
time, only some discoloured shabbiness of limp
damask. The Green Room, next door, had equally
outlived its name; but the Green Room, at this
uncertain hour, was full of dark shadow, and its
colour was quenched in ominous depths. It seemed
as mysterious as a cavern, rather long and low; the
oblong of the triple window, at the further end, was
wreathed about with heavy leafage, black by this

time in the solemn evening. Out there the night was gathering quickly. The Green Room, like most of the rooms at Earlham, was full of troubling doors, concealing cupboards and recesses like vaults. On no account open that one, to the left; something might easily steal behind you as you did so, thrust you into the blackness and bolt the door upon you; reason is shaken at the thought. But this one to the right—fling it open and see. It might lead into just another dark pit; but you get a pleasing surprise. The western twilight meets you; the door leads into a little dressing-room, a powder-closet, that fills the second of the two ancient gables; here there is still a remnant of day, sinking beyond the distant river, down there in the park, and the low swell of the trees on the sky-line. The mist creeps and crawls in streamers up the slope from the river. Night is upon us, and very soon there resounds through the house the booming crescendo of the dinner-gong.

So the company and the quality drew together and departed to their meal, their " late dinner "; and the tone of the upper regions of the house was changed. It must have been nearly bed-time, but there seem to have been delays and interludes. A spirit of merry informality ranged about the passages, and I catch sight of the bright faces of the ministering maids at their work, passing from room to room. The passages were dimly lighted with a very small oil-lamp in a corner, here and there; the maids had their flat brass candle-sticks, with snuffers and flaring tapers of tallow. One follows them about, hilariously helping and hindering, and of course it is an interlude to be protracted by all possible arts. To the nursery, however, one must presently gravitate; and there, perhaps, our grandmother's body-maid sits by this time with her workbasket under the lamp. More talk, more human gaiety—but it cannot last much longer; and then one is shelved out of sight once more, put away in the blank silence of the Eleven-sided Room.

15

How the days revolve—they are always ending in painful shadow, always beginning in a dance and flutter of sunshine; and yet they are endless too, with vast unbroken tracts of occupation between waking and sleeping. There was a rhythm of life that oscillated from the nursery, the upper rooms and our dear friends at work there—from these to the other world, the world of our grandparents and uncles and cousins, and back again. The swing of the day was now in this direction, now in that— with the bright attic-room in the top passage, and the welcome of the loving old nurse with her soft eyes and cheeks, as the centre where everything converged and met. That was a spot by itself, where all movement flowed and was stilled, all interests were mingled. But elsewhere a child, free, and so very free, of both worlds, distinguished clearly between the two; each had its own fine zest and savour. Nobody could say that one was better or less good than another, where both were so richly endowed; and nobody could think of them save as utterly distinct and diverse.

Could I not mark the very point of transition?

I can easily do so by beginning from the moment when we slip out of the big dining-room, leaving our elders still over their breakfast. The heavy door swings in my hand, while the mild voice of our grandfather is heard calling down the table to ask whether any one is " going in " this morning (to Norwich, that is); and then the door shuts behind me, as that door always would, with its peculiar soft thunder, echoing along the bit of curved passage that leads to the hall. Full of light, hung with engravings of clerical portraits and an old print of Norwich city with its church-towers, this short corridor bends into the hall, deserted for the moment; and quickly we are upon the shallow stair-case and sidling up its low wooden balustrade. One flight, another, and then there is a landing, and a vista before you of a long dim passage, with a window at the far-away end of it. But here on the open landing I can linger, I can loiter and stare into the glass cases of stuffed birds, several of them, tier upon tier—young owls crowding and peering out of a hole in a mossy tree-trunk, a colony of ruffs and reeves, a pair of great herons, best of all, arching their necks over a family of alert-eyed nestlings. Can I ever pass these striking creatures without stopping to examine them one by one, deepening the pleasant impression of their looks and attitudes, though I have long known them all by heart? And then in a trice—here is a friend with her brooms and dusters, appearing out of the dim passage and turning into one of the bed-rooms with the mirthful flash of a smile at us; and the oddest change takes place in the mood of life. Down in the dining-room

66

it was all very gay and interesting—but even perilously interesting, one might feel; there is always an element of the unaccountable in one's elders, so it would seem, and something fearful in the confidence and readiness of their jesting talk; it is great, but there is a touch, a tang, as Browning says, of something that is not wholly ease. Above-stairs, on the other hand, hanging upon our friend's skirt while she sprinkles the passage-floor with damp tealeaves and brooms them before her like sea-weed on a beach—who can deny that there is here a strain of freedom to which one returns with relief? Above-stairs, after all, there is a Bohemian fling of jollity and levity which nobody can fail to appreciate; this is no mere brilliant spectacle, it is life itself.

In a society so humane as that of the household at Earlham a child could expand, unfold, find free and independent expression. It is part of a liberal education, and the company in the drawing-room and the dining-room can never quite supply it. The life of our elders is really a performance, a show for our benefit; we look on with delight, and yet there seems to be a need of self-protection. You cannot give yourself entirely away; for even to the most benevolent of uncles and cousins you are a child, a member of the class of children. Perfect freedom begins when you stand completely on your own feet, an individual being. And that is what you become, once among these friends upstairs; the change is unmistakable. You take your own line, you crack your own jokes, you say what you think; and the only drawback is that now and then you are tempted above yourself, you try to be funnier still, and then everything goes strangely wrong. A moment ago it was all brave and splendid with adventurous humour; and now a chill strikes in, a kind of forlornness, against which you struggle reckless and loud. But it is vain; the humour of the scene is scraped and rasped, it ends in exasperation. That happens occasionally, and then, no doubt, you feel the attraction of order and style, in scenes where the art of living is thoroughly mastered and controlled. It is social training, however, all of it together, and you cannot afford to miss the experience of either world.

16

The art of living, I always felt, was magnificently practised by our uncles. There were not a few of them, and the house would have been incomplete indeed without the sound of their striding steps about the passages. They came and went, some or others of them were always at Earlham as I think of the place. In later years I discovered that they were young, but in those early days they were tremendously mature and manly, and it was clear to us that their youth was far behind them. They were twenty, five-and-twenty, thirty years old perhaps; but there is no count of ages upon the plane of maturity, none is older or younger than another. Above them, in quite a different category, is the plane of extreme old age, where our grandparents were; they, I suppose, might be on the further side of sixty. On the ordinary, intervening levels of grown-up life the question does not arise; every one has ceased to be young, no one can imaginably grow old.

INDOORS

I do not wish to deny that I was afraid of our uncles; I would not assertively have crossed their paths, not for a large reward. When one of them came tramping mightily down the passage, with a round Shakespearian trolling of song and laughter, I should wish to make myself very small indeed, to slip round a corner, out of sight, with a casual air. There is no need to be ashamed of the impulse; it is not a weakly, unimaginative fear. It is rather the sense of a great deficiency, a want of presence and weight and stature, moral rather than physical. If the Great Mogul came suddenly swinging into the room, with kindly careless patronage and a gleam of ironic mockery, should you feel entirely at ease, ready to answer back with freedom? Not so—you would find yourself embarrassed, thinly giggling and tittering, and it would be a relief when the splendid visitor lounged away and left you to yourself.

But if it should be possible to watch the play of so much humour and experience from some safe entrenchment, to look on unseen, at any rate unremarked—then indeed the opportunity would be seized and enjoyed. There must always, as I said, be some slight thrill of risk in the exposure to such a spectacle, for these elemental forces are incalculable. It is well worth an occasional discomfiture, however, to have the sight of our uncles in their leisure, when the hail of their wit is falling upon each other, or when they are brilliantly attacking and rallying their parents. It is beyond belief how entertaining they can be. At luncheon, especially —for of course we lunch with our elders in the

69

dining-room—there are times when the amusement is an ecstasy; nobody would guess how deeply the rapture of appreciation is flooding the listener's soul, screened behind a pair of staring eyes that travel intently from speaker to speaker. Perhaps it is betrayed now and then by an uncontrollable escape of laughter, but generally it is too full for sound; laughter is distracting, and the whole of one's attention is swallowed by the scene. Years and years afterwards it is as new in the memory as ever; the light words that were thrown to and fro by a party of genial young men in holiday mood, carelessly thrown and forgotten—not one of them is lost; they were engraved for good and all upon adamantine tables, the mind of a child.

As I slipped out of the dining-room just now, along the short curve of the passage where the clerical portraits clattered on the wall in the summer breeze, I passed the door of the school-room, so called, the room where in these days our uncles smoked and congregated and trailed their long legs over the chairs. If the door is open I catch the pleasant old staleness of tobacco which always lingered there—there, and nowhere else in the house—and a glimpse of the negligent masculine litter of books, papers, pipes, upon the square table and the window-seats. You drop down a step as you enter; it is a small wainscoted parlour, with its woodwork glazed and grained in the perverse manner that ruled throughout the house. This, I see, was the room in which the author of Lavengro was entertained, long ago, by old Joseph John; it must have been this room, though in fact it has two windows, and no old elm can ever have shaded them from without. They open on to a slip of flower-garden, enclosed between the two wings of the dining-room and the drawing-room; and in morning hours, before the sun is on this side of the house, a fresh fragrance of dewiness and earthiness floats into the room, mingling with the tobacco-smoke.

But I am far, I need not say, from making free with this sanctum of our uncles; not without special encouragement should I go plumping down that step from the passage into the school-room. I waver about in the offing when our grandmother looks in upon them with an affectionate glance and word, takes the opportunity of opening a window (shut again, no doubt, when her back is turned), and protests, in answer to an enquiry, that she is really resting in her room. "What was that we heard about your resting after lunch?" She would smile back upon the demand with a tender admiring look at the large soldier-son, severely confronting her. "Yes, dear, I *am* resting!"—but her eye would be caught by a table to be tidied, a chair to be shifted, and she would pause and begin to occupy herself. Doing other people's work for them, as usual, when she ought to be resting—that was a frequent charge; her sons would not be slow to intercept her. If the books were all on the floor and a pair of coffee-cups in an arm-chair, it was where they were meant to be; she was on no account to move them. Foiled, amused, tenderly smiling, she would pass out; and nobody supposed that she would reach her room without bethinking herself of this or that undone, to be attended to on the spot. She would next be discovered, it was likely, in the " poor people's cupboard "—a scrap of a room, upstairs, given over to a store of blankets and shawls and petticoats—rummaging out a gift for the bed-ridden old friend she would be visiting that afternoon.

She was incorrigible, she always escaped the vigilance of her sons; but they were unremitting. On Sundays in particular, in the long hot summer evening, the question of church-going was acute. The family party, as I happen to see it, is scattered about in the coolness of the hall, watchful to see that our grandmother, if she *will* go journeying off through the level blaze to Colney church, shall at least take the carriage and drive thither. " Too hot, too hot for you to walk," they say; " and why not stay at home under the trees ? " That couldn't be ; but she made the concession of taking the carriage, promising herself to justify it by stopping on the way to pick up infirm old Mrs. Brown or weak-kneed old Mrs. Giles, for the treat of evening service. So she drove away, and the family loitered in idleness ; and presently, of all surprising sights, there was the carriage returning, just when service would be beginning, with our grandmother still in it. I hear the note of triumph from her sons as she re-joined the party—she had thought better of it, then ! It was quite a little gay scene while she explained ; poor old Mrs. Giles had said No, she didn't want to go to church, not at all—and that good Eliza Cope-man, a reliable vocalist, had been found already there in her place, prepared to lead the hymns—

" and so I came back," said our grandmother, and the moment is fixed in my mind by the light pretty chime of self-satisfaction in her voice, conscious as she is that she has obeyed her children's wish, and yet obeyed it in her own way, by a free decision. So everybody is pleased, and one of our uncles sends her into a ripple of mirth by his rich enactment of old Mrs. Giles—but indeed I must let the momentary jest lie quiet, after the third part of a century. It is too small to bring from so far, though I possess it intact.

17

I seem to have wandered over most of the house, but I have rather carefully kept away from a part of it. I never knew such a house for refusing to fit compactly into the space between its walls and the roof and the ground; the inhabited rooms appear to overflow it in some quarters, and to fall strangely short in others. How was it, for example, that the pleasant scullery, which lay far away in the out-buildings of the back-yard, had doubled and screwed itself round so sharply that its window looked full into the flower-beds by the garden-door? It was impossible to make the building, as you explored it within, square with its aspect from without; and while at one end the scullery behaved like a house through the looking-glass, at the other there were whole regions that were lost, that bulked largely in the outer structure and disappeared when you sought them indoors.

I happen to know, however, where a part of them are to be found. There would be many a morning

73

when I chance to be hovering betimes about the
hall, while the butler and his underling are setting
out the benches for prayers; and then I get a sight
of the great grey Bluebeard chamber from which
they are brought forth. Stone steps, behind a door
in the corner by the wide fire-place, lead downward
into this lost abode. It cannot be called a cellar,
for it has a window above the level of the geranium
border outside; but the light that trickles in there
is spare and sour with dust, and whenever you
venture down the stone steps you feel as though
you were the first to stumble upon a forgotten
apartment, sealed and abandoned long ago for a
sufficient reason. It would not surprise me to find
it hung with threadbare finery, and a table covered
with the mouldering remains of a wedding-feast,
and even a gaunt old figure in a bridal veil and
yellowing satin at the head of it; not for nothing
have I read of Miss Havisham, in that first thrill of
a plunge into the world of Dickens, and she readily
takes her place in the lathe-room. It was called
the lathe-room; one of our uncles or great-uncles,
I suppose, had once fitted it as a work-shop. But
now it was only a store-room, a wilderness of old
lumber, made sinister by the grey twilight and the
silent chill that reigned there even at highest noon;
and the very thought of the dim unexplained
objects, piled up, standing there in that fallen day,
has an influence that strikes me solemn.

Moreover it could not escape me that this tomb-
like space was only the beginning of a whole range
of such apartments. There was still a large quarter
of the house, the big panelled ante-room and the

arm of the drawing-room beyond it, which actually had no inhabited ground-floor at all; and fancy runs riot in picturing the derelict saloons and galleries that may yawn beneath the floor we tread. There is room for I know not how many secret chambers, hidden away in echoing blackness; nothing betrays them outside, for in this quarter a couple of apparent windows, facing upon the gravel-sweep of the front door, prove to be blank and blind, glass panes with only the darkened wall behind them. I can imagine what I please, therefore—I could then and I still can, for I find that to the last I never penetrated the mystery of those forgotten spaces.

But rather let me turn to more comfortable associations—to the sun-bright scullery, perhaps, where such remarkable operations were conducted, the groundwork of Mrs. Chapman's beautiful art. The children looked on, no doubt, with clear-eyed interest while her hand-maids set her palette, as you may say, prepared the raw material for her creative touch. They plucked and chopped, they hacked and scraped—so it comes back to me; the lovely dish on the table in the dining-room has a strange past behind it, if you knew, full of bald and uncompromising detail. I could mention a few facts in the history of the roast chicken off which we lunch— but it is odd how people prefer to blink these things. Surely it is interesting to know that when Maggie is going to cook a chicken she first plucks it, then she scoops out its —— and that is as far as I get in the story, when I produce it at the luncheon-table, for my squeamish elders set up a hoot that cuts me short. She does, anyhow; and I can watch her with absorption while she makes an excellent job of it. Nearly always there is something queer and notable going forward in the scullery, and Maggie faces the facts of the case like a sensible realist.

But Mrs. Chapman's art is naturally upon a higher plane. There is a rare charm in the look of the kitchen, her studio—bright and lofty, with two large windows on one side of it, another at the end. The flags of the floor are crisp to the tread, the dressers shine with their pots and pans, the huge table is scrubbed to the whiteness of paper. The racks and gratings and oven-doors of the range, with the little furnace roaring in the midst of them, are infinitely suggestive; before every meal the artist is engaged in an enchanting game with this magnificent toy. Imagine the delight—but her rare skill does not reveal itself in broad touches, emphatic manipulations, such as are to be observed in the scullery; these higher refinements are proved but in the eating. There indeed they were recognized, they were acclaimed; upon many of them I should like to dwell minutely. All the mellow ripeness of a bountiful harvest, all the light wild savours of spring, were caught and mingled in the artistry of this remarkable woman—I feel sure of it. There was a heart of noble staunchness in her masterpieces, and a soul of unnameable fragrance. But the genius of a cook is fugitive as that of an actor, a dancer. What do we know of the grace of Taglioni? We have only another's word for it, and for the perfection of Mrs. Chapman's accomplishment I can only offer mine.

INDOORS

Now and then she would invite us to tea, a grand tea in The Room. In The Room, her private and anonymous parlour, a wondrous table would be spread; I remember the dazed impression, as one entered, of dishes and dishes high-piled, profusion and variety in which the mind was lost. The Room, like the scullery, had the odd property of wriggling itself into an unexplained position, revealed when you looked from the window. It was approached from the kitchen-passage, which lay far off and away from the garden-door and the lawn; yet there was the lawn, full in front of the window, and it never seemed clear how it had arrived in that quarter. Earlham always remained an experience, the house was a condition of things through which one moved, inhaling enchantment; it did not exist, it hardly does so now, as an object detached, imagined, ensphered in thought. I chance upon The Room in the course of my wanderings, and the small surprise of seeing the familiar flower-beds just there, under the window, is punctually renewed.

But enough, the table is dazzling in its abundance, for our good friend's notion of a fit repast is indeed superb. Shall I describe it in detail?—is it not a pity that the memory should perish, when it might be chronicled to the last minuteness? At any rate I must say that the freshness and firmness, the cool succulence and the sherry-coloured gleam of *these*—these here, stacked upon their dish, arresting the vagrant eye—will represent the cynosure of the feast; and to these at least you must do justice, where it is impossible to do justice impartially over all the table. In an hour's time—be certain that

77

we are not to be hurried—we shall look round us
with regret, I dare say, at chances wasted and lost;
for even the greediest have never kept pace with
Mrs. Chapman's inspiration. But of these in their
builded pile, a hollow and four-square tower of
them, I well engage that no trace will be left when
at last the company disperses.

18

Suddenly, as it seems, I find myself alone, quite
alone in the house, in the deep of the soundless
afternoon. An extraordinary stillness fills the hall,
where I pause almost in awe; the garden-door
stands open, and nothing is heard but the light flap
of the awning which hangs in the doorway. Why or
where all the family has scattered I could not say,
or how it is that I am loitering solitary at this hour,
half-shy of the silence; but I guess that I have
strayed in from the garden—and yes, I see how
it would happen. Ranging along the gravel walk
outside, one would drift towards the door and the
porch, because the cream-coloured plaster and paint
of the porch has an attraction. By this time of
day the surface is hot, really scorching hot in the
sun, and it is pleasant to lay a hand upon the
plaster and to feel how it burns; it positively burns
your palm. And then I might hitch aside the
striped awning and meet the sudden stillness and
dimness of the house within, the cool quietude
secretly stored away there while the full-throated
blaze of August beats on it from without. It would
be enough to give me pause; the house, so entered,
is like a great cave, on the narrow mouth of which

one has stumbled by chance, unexpectedly. I should certainly be drawn in; and there I am in the middle of the bare floor, wondering at the solitude.

I hear how my footsteps sounded as I crossed to the flight of the stairs. Just there stood the great dinner-gong, and with the touch of a knuckle I might wake a low reverberation—a light touch, only enough to start the hollow murmur very gently. It said plainly that I had the house to myself; a small echo like this, of a powerful voice barely breathing into sound, seems to steal away into all the deserted rooms and to reveal their emptiness. I could be entirely conscious of the spell of the house at such a moment; it was romance—romance that I just can, just cannot, define in words. I can detect the mingling of many influences; but each of them shifts out of the line of sight as I turn to fix it. They could flutter and charm the mind of a child— no doubt of that; a surge of excitement would carry the child up the shallow stairs, treading on air. It seemed like an immense expansion of one's power, an annihilation of limits, with a warm gush of new freedom that might easily set the heart thumping unawares. That house, those rooms, Earlham the well-beloved, a place all steeped in its beautiful golden past—such images advance like an invasion into a mind too small to hold them—too small, but that it suddenly opens wide, arches out, ready, one would say, to contain a world. It is a great experience, flashing into a life that is always so busy with small immediate tangible things; at Earlham, especially, there was seldom a moment unclaimed by the sight and sound, the smell and touch and taste of the eventful surface. Year by year as we returned thither for the perfect weeks of summer, there was an ever-increasing hoard of familiar detail to be re-discovered and examined and brooded upon; many long days could be spent, I almost think, in simply travelling over the texture of the place, inch by inch, to make sure that it was all as one very well knew it to be. But then came a moment, like this in which I find myself alone, when the imagination seemed to shoot up all-powerful, masterfully enlarging the capacity of one's thought and reaching out to invisible wonders.

Forgetting my occupation in the garden, whatever it was, I reach the top of the first short flight of stairs, where I face the open doorway of the ante-room. Not a sound, not a soul; and in the northern greyness of the ante-room the solitude is intensely solemn. I have mentioned the dais and the bow-window, the great china jar and the green window-seat; but let me try to describe more closely what I see. I stand on the threshold, and I look across the width of the room; its length lies to my right, with the bow-window at the end of it, and the greenery of the lime-avenue outside. Exactly opposite to me there is another window, facing west; so that at this end of the room a mellower light is shed upon the green carpet—not enough, however, to scatter widely, or to tinge the pallor of the northern day which mainly occupies the space. But is that clear? There is some kind of a picture in your mind, as I place the words; and it is utterly unlike the picture that *I* possess, and the finest art in the world could not set yours right in every detail. I wish I could see at least your mistakes, to correct them; it is disheartening, no less, to stand here on the threshold of the ante-room with everything so plainly before me, and to know that the accuracy of my vision is of no avail. I might just as well have forgotten, just as well *not* know the look and colour and feel of every object in the room almost, for all the power my knowledge gives me to make a complete and faithful report. Something is sure to go wrong in the impression I give; and it will be sketchy, cloudy, vague, compared with the impression I retain.

In telling an imaginary story a writer is content to leave the reader in his error. The reader imagines the house, the room, the garden, as he pleases; what matter if it is all distorted, re-arranged, so long as certain few details are correctly placed? An old-fashioned room, a window-seat, some high-backed chairs, some portraits on the panelled walls —enough, there is a setting for the blush-tinted maiden who gazes from the window, a letter just falling from her hand. So the story might begin, and the author would contentedly leave you to fill in the picture of the room as you choose—with a thousand points of unlikeness to the room as he thought of it. But in a true story, like mine, everything seems to be spoilt if you deviate from my memory at any point—if you place, for example, the wrong kind of Chinese cups and beakers on the cabinet, if you omit the little cluster of humming-birds under their glass dome on the table, if you are confused on the subject of the green roses in the carpet; and even now you do not know where the cabinet stood, or how the humming-birds were flanked by the other objects on that table. Not one of them strikes me as unessential to the effect that I should wish to evoke.

It cannot be helped, I must leave it imperfect and uncertain. Myself, as I write the words, I pass up the length of the room and silently note what I see, exalted by my sense of power and illumination. Alone with the house, alone with its watchful spirit, one is stirred with vast, delicious apprehension; the stretch of a pair of arms seems to grow till one might touch the ceiling, the trees, the sky with a lifted hand. Indeed I feel like a ghost—I mean that the child so felt. I speak of the spirit of the house, not knowing what words to use; but to the child who wanders up the room, who mounts the step of the dais (slipping on the treacherous rug that is spread there), who stops to peer into the great jar and smell the rose-leaves, who lingers handling and caressing the pointed knob of the lid—to the child it is no matter for such a simple phrase. It is far profounder, more complicated. It is I, it is the child who is in the spirit, miraculously pervading the good old earthly presence of the place, the house; I am well away and apart from that figure by the china jar. The figure turns and moves; mechanically it plunges its fingers into the fragrant dust of roses and spices; but I must have strayed very far from it, have lost sight of it entirely, for I have the oddest difficulty in getting back again when I must.

Some one comes into the room, the solitude is broken; and my wandering fancy is recalled to the body it had forgotten. But there is a strange interval in which the creature, the empty body, actually speaks and answers of its own accord, looking and sounding as though I were there to direct it. I see it and hear it, all helplessly; it is surprising that the new-comer notices nothing, takes the mechanical image for myself. It is uncomfortable, it is awkward; and the disconcerted spirit makes an effort, quite painful, to wrench itself back into its rightful place. You know the sensation, I don't doubt; the child I speak of was often plagued by it, and the memory chances to be linked with the thought of that slippery step of the dais in the ante-room, the green-grey light, the surge of the humming of bees in the limes. It passes, it passes; the spirit is suddenly restored to the body, and I pick up the thread of the casual talk as though nothing had happened. But would it not be in such minutes as these, now and then renewed, that the child could learn the meaning of a romantic passion?

Earlham was the centre of many loves, much tender and grateful loyalty; from far back its sons and daughters had given it of their best. They grew up there and went their ways, they came back with children of their own, they were drawn always nearer to the place by their memories of youth and age. The bond was strengthened by joy, by sorrow; so much they had seen there, birthdays and merry-making, high hopes, the tracks of time, the apparition of easeful death, that the house became like a part of themselves, they might feel that their experience was embodied in its walls and timbers. Yes, but Earlham was as much and as dear, it seems to me, even to a child who looked back over a hand's-breadth, a little patch of summertime that it amazes me now to measure from a distance. How many times, returning to Earlham, had I rushed to the window-seat of faded velvet, clambered to the ledge of the window, hung there to survey the weeping ash in the grassy enclosure beneath?—punctually one greets the dome of the weeping ash again, that so habitable tree, as shapely as a bell-tent. Already the vista of an age was behind me, I should have said; and if I could remember three years or four—four wonderful August evenings on which we returned to Earlham again as of old—that would then be the utmost, I suppose, the full stretch of my conscious knowledge of the place. Back there as I now am, in that particular hour of thrilled solitude, I taste a passion that I cannot recognize as the bright holiday romance of a child; it has solemn depths, as though it could already be charged with a richly mingled experience.

Indeed there is no count of time in the life of an imagination; from the moment it is touched you are freed from the necessity of earning your experience grain by grain, in the common fashion. For days and days you may work patiently forward, appropriating the spoil of the moment, adding it to your store; if you are exceedingly careful and attentive your pile may be always increasing, a day's work may respectably heighten it. But it only grows with the measure of time, a few shining specks to the hour perhaps; there is no hastening or rushing the process so long as it is left in your hands. And then in a flash it is out of your hands, and everything happens in new ways. Sight becomes more than seeing, becomes a faculty that enfolds and embraces, in one stroke possessing itself of the scene that till now you have plodded over with thin senses unaided. To see, to touch, by ordinary laws, is to retain but a point at a time—just the point where you glanced or where your finger fell; weeks of toil it might easily take to acquire and assimilate a scene in that manner. But the imagination, unaccountably stirred, sweeps forward with a sudden billowy swing, gathers an armful in the tick of a moment—and there, before you can wink an eye, is your small laborious treasure increased a hundredfold. If the work of days, of weeks, is achieved while a dew-drop runs over a leaf (like Meredith's " bloom of dawn "), do not doubt that there is room for a life-time in the memory of a child—a child for whom the flash of illumination has fallen now and then in the hush of an August afternoon.

" Of thee to say Behold, has said Adieu ": it is true of the rose-glimmer of dawn, it is truer still, I am sorry to find, of these beautiful visitations. Somebody came into the room, common life shut down upon the child again—so it happened; but so it always happens, I have never discovered the secret of prolonging the few rare moments. Enough that in passing they bestow their imperishable gift; the time, the place, are marked for ever afterwards, plainly to be seen over lengthening years. I am sure it is impossible to forget them—even when at last there are some that shine at a very far distance, like this of the great cool ante-room at Earlham.

85

The remembrance hangs there, beaconing clearly, a long way off by this time; it is safe from all chances, it will only quaver and sink when the child is extinguished too.

19

I cannot tear myself away; I loiter interminably across the green roses of that carpet, always trying to utter the sweet old memories that go rippling and beating in my brain. It is hard enough to describe what is before my eyes—the queer broad sofa or couch, for instance, covered with floriferous wool-work, so broad that you roll and roll I know not how many times, over and over, to get from one side to the other; but how much harder to catch these wafts and puffs of sensation that beset me while I veer to and fro, gradually making my way down the length of the room. There is a distinction, you see, between remembering, recalling things in detachment, recounting the tale of them —between this and recovering how it felt, how it was, when the things themselves were all about you, tacitly assumed and taken for granted. I might make a fair picture of the great angular couch (can I indeed omit it?), and I might shew how our bright-haired cousin, she of the lovely stories, joined us gaily and riotously in a game that sprawled over the expanse of it; but I am tormented by the sidelong influences of the scene, welling into it from right and left, which are not to be caught in a description of the scene itself. I forget them, perhaps, when I begin to make my picture; I think only of the absurd piece of furniture, hard and comfortless, suitable for nothing but to roll upon, and I recall its carved wooden frame and the bunched flowers of the wool-work;—and there, suddenly the air of the old day comes surging round me, and yes, I say to myself, that is how it was, how it felt.

How can one talk about Earlham to any purpose, unless to the picture of things seen and done it is possible to add this aura of sweet sensation? Even as I hang on the sharp edge of the couch, where it is framed in the band of wooden carving, I am aware of the savours, echoes, rhythms of Earlham all about me—I don't know which is the word for them. Evidently the air must be full of them; and they vary, what is more, from room to room, for nobody could mistake the mood, the tone of the ante-room or confuse it with any other. What is it, then? How ridiculous to perceive it so acutely, and yet to be quite unable to name it—a matter of such definite qualities too, nothing uncertain or dim. All I can say is that as soon as I enter this room there is something in my hollow footfall (it sounded hollow and muffled, just across the threshold), in the soft smell of the velvet curtains, in the peculiar rake of the two lights, the northern and the western, in the clean brownness of the high panels (stained and grained, you remember)—some influence in all these which affects and qualifies anything I may say or do, see or hear, between these four walls. Cross over to the other door, enter the drawing-room beyond, and behold what a change in the spirit and the climate. It is another world, with another fine rain of delicate emanations—I feel them intensely, as soon as ever I turn the corner of the leather screen by the door. Here, for instance, I pause for a moment by the round table, the table with its black and yellow cover, on which there stood (shadowed by the bowery bouquet of dahlias and asparagus) a sort of dish or tray of clouded marble, supported on metal feet and garnished with little chains and dangling balls—perhaps it had been bought at the Great Exhibition. Now mark, I swing one of the little chains so that its marble ball strikes the dish—*clink*! And if that is not enough, I turn to one of the candlesticks on the— the chiffonier, would it be called?—and set the glass lustres gently clanking; and this at any rate gives me the note of the drawing-room in a trice. Clink, clank; the soft voices ring out; and listening to them now, with eyes shut, I know beyond doubt that I am in the drawing-room at Earlham.

So it goes, from room to room; round every corner there is a change of atmosphere, instant and complete, each with its penetrating appeal. Never for a moment have I confused them; and I test my clear knowledge by brushing swiftly back through the ante-room, up the next flight of stairs, along the passage, and opening a door or two at random, left and right. This is the door that leads to the back-stairs, where the boards are bare and resonant; or this again is the dark entry through which one fumbles into the Blue Room, where the low window-seats command a view of the front door, and you hear the crisp crackle of the gravel under the carriage-wheels; and here is the nursery once more, where each of the five doors shuts on a different note, a click or a thud, sharply distinguished; and in fine there is no possibility of mistaking the changes of pitch (that is the word, I think, after all) to which the regions of the house are variously attuned. No account of Earlham could satisfy me which failed to mark these deep distinctions, failed to make them heard and felt in every scene; and it means that I can be satisfied by no account whatever, or by none but that which memory is always at hand to compose, speaking to every sense at once. When we have learned to create pictures of music, symphonies of fragrance, honey-draughts of colour and form, and all in a single achievement of art, then we may hope for an artist with the genius of memory—not till then.

20

But come, after long rambling and roaming I must plant myself firmly on the spot where I began. I was on one of the red seats in the hall, watching the household file into their places for prayers; and then came the hymn, the chapter, the exposition of the chapter, and the appealing cadences of our grandfather's voice while he prayed. As we rose to our feet after the final moments of silence, the stirring and shuffling and bustling of life went forward again; the benches were swept off into their dim hiding-place, an uncle or two went bounding upstairs, I dare say, to revise a vamped toilet, the rest of the company strayed to the garden-door and the twinkling flower-beds that flanked it outside. I myself had been out there already, before prayers; for I remember that as I sat in one of the side-arches of the shallow porch, dangling my legs, a packet of letters had fallen with a plop on the gravel from an upper window. It always happened so, in the half-hour before prayer-time; grandmother's window was just overhead, and when she had read her letters she bunched them together and dropped them on to the gravel by the porch, for grandfather to pick up and read as he returned from an early stroll. He greeted us, where we sat and drummed our heels, with a kindly quizzical gleam. " Good-morning, sir ; good-morning, miss ; how do you do, this bow-tiful morning " —he had a pleasant way of so sounding the first syllable of the word, like *beau* in French. He picked up the packet of letters and passed into the study, and then it was soon time for his congregation to assemble.

The children had breakfasted earlier, in the bright nursery, but they were quite ready to follow their elders to the dining-room, on the signal of the gong. There were peaches, there were grapes, pears, plums ; and if our elders were busy with their own meal at first, we could hover and range around till our turn came. At the further end of the room there stood a miniature billiard-table, which kept us occupied ; the balls spun and flew on the green cloth till they crashed—crashed on the polished boards of the floor, and warning voices called us to order. Or we might linger expectant by our grandmother—and her manner of treating a meal was always interesting. In front of her was the great pot-bellied silver kettle on its foliated stand ; it was a kettle that sat down comfortably, with the figure of an Indian

god. She began to fill a tea-cup—but stay, she saw
our grandfather busy with the dishes that were
ranged before him at his end of the table; he was
serving the company with his neat precision; and
" Will you have some of this, dear ? " he called
to her, spoon in hand. " Not so much—*half* that "
—her protest flew back before his spoon could
touch the dish; vivid in her mind was the horror of
a " great helping." " Such a great slice," she
declared, as the meal of a wren was placed before
her; and the tea-cup was filled, but not before she
had swiftly divided her scrap of bacon and deposited
most of it on the plate of her neighbour. It was
all very agreeable to watch, so instinct with life;
I could stare most contentedly, and it was splendid
when she roused one of her sons, stirring him to
rich rejoinder, by some infringement on his rights
and liberties. Did he appear to be wastefully,
recklessly shovelling the jam or the butter on his
plate? Well, she couldn't help it, the word escaped her; and then you should have seen the
grand humour of his remonstrance. They delighted
to challenge her precious minute economies, to tell
how she would travel from the furthest end of the
house to light her candle at the kitchen fire, sooner
than strike a valuable match; she denied it, but
she could not quite positively deny it, and her
pretty smile, at once submitting, protesting, appealing, beamed gently as she turned again to her
tea-making. What a dear little drama of character
—just the kind of scene that would hold us
entranced, while the biggest peach was being peeled
for us.

EARLHAM

Our grandfather had finished his breakfast, had announced that he should be " going in " that morning, had disappeared from the room; and our grandmother was busy in the background, unobtrusively—she was clearly making up a parcel (goodness knows what went into it) for grandfather to leave at some humble door in Norwich, but she didn't wish to call ribald attention to it. The rest of the party lounged about the long table, expansively jesting and talking; and it was a moment of the day that concerned us, for plans might be broached, there might be talk of an excursion on the river, a picnic. And anyhow it was the moment when the possibilities of the day began to open and extend before us; and when I think of the incalculable spaciousness of the day, a prospect that disappeared over the horizon without a hint of a night or another day beyond it, I cannot wonder that I seemed to have just as much life behind me at that hour as ever in later years. Such immensities of time in a single day—even if there were only a few hundreds of days bestowed away in my memory, they stretched the count of my years to a high figure. Did you ever feel young, at least till there began to be those who thought you old? Awkward, shapeless, inexpert I might feel, sometimes light and flimsy as fluff, sometimes ponderous as lead, but never in those days young; and evidently it is not surprising. This, however, was not the point at the moment; I was entirely engaged in considering whether it would be more perfect bliss to plunge into a morning in the garden, without our elders, or to learn that some of them were prepared to take us on the river, rowing down to Cringleford mill. Which should I choose to-day, if choose I might? Indeed I must have both, and I will very shortly —but not for a few minutes yet.

For look, I unexpectedly chance upon another small scene that detains me. I had quite forgotten it, but when we left the dining-room, the morning plan having been settled, and dashed away through the hall, we found our grandmother sitting on the red sofa by the staircase, talking to a young clerical gentleman, a curate, who was seated beside her. How should I know the subject of their talk? I couldn't say, but I was perfectly aware that the young curate was being " spoken to " about something—I don't know what, perhaps about his preaching, perhaps about his manner of drawling and droning through the service; anyhow our grandmother had been impelled, in her quick warm way, to speak a gentle word of warning and advice. Of course it was for grandfather to do this, really, if it had to be done, but he was so patient, so mild; he would have put up with the long-winded drawl, would never have noticed it perhaps; whereas to grandmother it was a vivid irritation from the first, and she was bound to take some step. I wish I might have heard what she actually said to the rather unkempt young man, when she drew him apart to speak her mind. Nobody could guess how she began—that was certain; probably there was a bewildered moment for the young man, a moment when there was a doubt, a wan light, a scare in his eye; how the first word of admonition would spring from her was never to be foretold, as we well knew. A little later, as I see them talking together upon the broad sofa, things are very different, the poor man's passing air of discomfiture has vanished entirely. By this time they are deep in converse, and the curate has revived and expanded; I catch the tones of our grandmother's voice, warm and fervent, with a little break in it that is eloquent of christian sympathy and feeling. They are far beyond the small matter of reproof, whatever it was, and the young man responds to her lead with eagerness; when she was moved (and so easily she was moved) to the expression of her heart of piety, there was a soaring lift in her voice that inspired a listener, that caught him up to the mood of her ardent self-forgetful sincerity. So by this time their converse has winged away from petty things, and the young man's confidence is renewed, and he follows her with admiring enthusiasm. His look of veneration, her rapt uplifted eyes, give me an abiding impression in the five seconds that it takes to cross the hall and gain the staircase.

We were " getting ready to go out," and surely it is odd that the process should take so long. You would think that to seize a hat (if so much as a hat) and fly to the garden-door could be done in a stroke; what more was there to do? But somehow there were delays and impediments. Between the foot of the stairs and the first landing, for instance, one might drop into a chasm of forgetfulness; one's purpose would suddenly vanish, melting away at the sight of those splendid stuffed herons, for the thousandth time, where they stood throwing out their great beaks so nobly over their nest. There

94

were four or five young ones in the nest, and there
was a sea-green egg unhatched—not very true to
nature perhaps, on the whole, for the nest lay upon
the bare ground, and there was no attempt at
scenery save for the sky and white clouds that were
painted on the back of the case. They had been
stuffed, those herons, in an uncritical age; but I
could easily supply the rocking tree-top, the whist-
ling wind. I knew where they came from, nest and
all—from no further off than the heronry in the
park at Earlham; we were immensely proud of the
heronry, which of course I shall visit before long.
I could not be sorry that one of the nests had once
been sacrificed, brought to ground, brought down
to my very feet; not otherwise is it given to one to
look down upon a sea-green heron's egg in its great
bowl of twigs; moreover I think there had been
some good reason for the extinction of this young
family—an accident to their parents, to their tree-
top, I forget what it was. And then the next case
above them, the strutting egregious ruffs, and the
owls in their hollow trunk—and I have tumbled
off into space and am lost, contemplating the owls,
when a voice, calling, reminds me of my purpose
and projects me forward on my way to the nursery.
It *does* take a long time to get ready. Half way
down the passage there is a step, edged with shining
brass; one takes a run at it, one jumps, crashing
upon the lower level; the impetus carries one past
the nursery door, to the window at the end of the
passage. Here there stood a species of fire-ex-
tinguisher, a thing of knobs and tubes and pump-
handles, which luckily served out its time without

ever being called into play; it stood idly upon the
window-seat, well placed for observation. But no
loitering now; back to the nursery—and I believe
I have not happened to mention the peculiarity of
the nursery door, this one of its five. It was double,
a door within a door, and between the two there
was a narrow dark space, just big enough to contain
me when both were shut. Stand in the space and
shut both the doors, and you are immured in a
black cell; for any one entering or leaving the
nursery unsuspectingly it is a fearful shock to
come upon you there, crouching for a spring. It
might be worth while to wait there for a minute,
very quietly, in case the nursery-maid should come
blundering in with a tray of crockery; she gives a
yelp and all but drops the tray, as you spring up
in her path. But forward, forward.

"Must I change my shoes? why need I? why?"
It appears that I am not rightly shod for messing
about in the garden. Isn't it unbelievable how the
superstition of changing, of substituting something
else for what you have on at the moment, clings to
the people about you? They cannot leave well
alone; and now it means having to thump my way
up the steep wooden stairs to the Eleven-sided
Room, after these shoes. But in the happy light of
morning the Eleven-sided Room, as I have said, is
a place of devious charm and interest. The strange
recesses and cupboards may be safely explored;
and as for the wall-paper of nursery rhymes, Mistress
Mary and Little Bo-peep and the rest of them in
endless repetition, really I think I could follow them
all round the eleven walls, reading each of the

legends a hundred times over. " With cockle-shells
and silver bells "—start from the corner where the
big card hangs (a card headed " Morning Hymn, by
John Keble "—which was faintly remarkable to me,
for Keble was a neighbouring farmer, and it was
difficult to think of him as the author of " New
every morning ")—start from this corner, I say,
and count how many times you can find the rhyme
of Mistress Mary repeated in the pattern of the
paper. You will lose count before long, I assure
you ; but no matter, here is the door of the odd
alcove above the wooden stairs, a door with a
square pane of glass in it, through which you may
boldly peer at this time of day. But really, these
intolerable shoes—drearily one faces the question
at last.

I should not like to say that I got ready without
further hitch. You never know where you may not
be tripped into that chasm of oblivious rumination,
contemplation, speculation ; it may yawn for you
at any point, at any time, along the passage and
down the stairs. But have I really dawdled for
long, after all ? I seem to be ready in a flash, to be
shooting across the hall to the garden-door. It
stands open as usual, and the awning lazily flaps
and bellies in the morning breeze.

II: IN THE GARDEN

IT was superb, the great lawn at Earlham—it really was. I have described how it was lifted up, almost to the level, I should think, of the first-floor windows, by a steep bank of shaven grass; but there was a considerable expanse on the lower level too, before you reached the bank. On this lower lawn, to right and left, there was a fantastic medley of flower-beds, cut in queer shapes, coils and lozenges and loops; and the gardener's fancy ran strangely riot, year by year, in selecting and disposing the flowers that filled them. Geraniums roasting-red, French marigolds orange and mahogany-coloured, the tomato-note of waxen begonias, exotic herbage all speckled and pied and ringstraked, dahlias, calceolarias—they were marshalled and massed together, they fought it out as they would. But indeed they were mastered by the sunshine, by the blaze of light in which they flashed and twinkled; and they fell back, right and left, leaving a wide space of clear clean grass unbroken. And then there rose before you the green bank, so steep that I wonder how the mowing-machine contrived to sidle along it and keep it thus smoothly shaven.

To me, as I gained the crest of the bank, it seemed as though the huge flat of the lawn stretched away and ahead for a mile; so serene, so steady and peaceful it was, with nothing to break its even greenness till the eye, sweeping far, reached the shrubberies and trees that bordered it about. The broad silence made nothing of such trivialities as a lawn-tennis net, a few croquet hoops; they were lost in the quiet plain. Beyond it the horizon was bounded by clumped oaks, by dim woods more distant; out there was the park, and you could catch sight of the cows swinging their tails in the deep pasture. On either hand was a dense thicket, with an edging of bright flowers—a straight edge, on this side and that, so that the lawn was a great square. From the further side of it the view of the house was beautifully mellow and kindly, with its long rows of old windows and its high chimney-stacks. But that comes later; at this hour of the morning I should not set out on the journey across the lawn; I should turn aside to the thickets and shrubberies, to the shadowy corners and recesses of which there were so many to choose from.

Turn, therefore, at the top of the bank, turn to the left and follow the edge of the slope till it brings you to this angle of the lawn; it is an excellent spot for the beginning of a morning's exploration. Many possibilities here converged; and here, to begin with, stood a wonderful white seat, semi-circular, triply divided, high in the middle and quite low at the sides—an ancient, a historic seat, on which I might well subside for a minute or so, while I try to explain the complication of interest that gathered in this corner. It is not easy at all; so much seems to happen at once, what with the geranium-blaze that here comes shelving up from

the lower level, and the red wall, with its cascade
of wistaria and clematis, that branches away from
a corner of the house and curves like an arm in this
direction, and the cool shrubbery rustling behind
me, and the glimpse, if I look round, of a sun-bright
enclosure, formally laid out, the approach to which
is just here, close at hand. It is difficult indeed to
make my way methodically; I should remain on
the white seat till nightfall, shifting from one to
another of its three divisions and back again, if
I had to describe how all these diversities fitted
together, conjoining at this point.

But there is no hurry, after all; and as I sit
there, under the tasselled branch of a larch that
leans out from the edge of the shrubbery, I take in
afresh the delightful sense of easy abundance, the
loose comfort, the soft-bosomed maturity of the
garden. Those lobelia-stripes, those marigold-
patches might look harsh and hard, you would
think; one knows how smartly odious they can
appear in a well-kept garden, so called, where the
flowers seem to have been—what shall I say?—to
have been stuffed and mounted, lest they should
take their ease as living creatures. Not a flower
could look constrained, unnaturally smartened, in
the garden at Earlham; even if they sat up in rows
and stripes, they did so with enjoyment uncon-
cerned. They glowed, they revelled; and moreover it was not, in any vulgar sense, a well-kept
garden. It was profusely inconsistent; if one
flower-bed was stuck all over with geraniums like a
pin-cushion and rimmed with horrible little mon-
sters of fretted, empurpled foliage, the next might

be a bower, a boscage, a ramp of sweet peas, a
bushy luxuriance of phlox and rosemary. And
especially the border against the slow curve of the
wall which I mentioned just now—this was a mazy
confusion of everything that gleams and glows and
exhales a spicery of humming fragrance. Peacock
butterflies, brilliant red admirals, fluttered over the
blue mist of sea-lavender; a tree of verbena, the
lemon-scented herb of which you pull a leaf whenever you pass, branched out close to the immense
old trunk of the wistaria; salvia blue and red,
bitter-sweet phloxes white and crimson-eyed, the
russet and purple trumpets of the lovely creature
afflicted with the name of salpiglossis, they all
rejoiced together, rambling and crowding in liberal
exuberance. The gardener might wreak his worst
will, scheming for a smart patchwork; but the free
soul of the garden escaped him and bloomed
tumultuously. Or rather, perhaps, there were
two souls in the gardener himself; one, a cramped
and professional soul, disliked and mistrusted a high-
spirited flower; but the other, more indulgent, had
the best of it in the garden.

By this time these southern flower-beds were
dry and warm; but in the shrubbery behind the
white seat the dew-fresh airs of early morning still
lingered. A path wandered off into the thicket, a
path with a smooth floor of beaten earth; and if
I should follow its twisting, in among the bushes of
laurel and snowberry, I should come upon a chill
little climate that stands like a wall, resisting the
shafts of warmth that steal in from outside. It is
amusing to feel the sharp, distinct edge of the

dankness which the sun has not reached as yet, and I might possibly spend some agreeable minutes in repeating the sensation; at one moment you are in southern softness, at the next you have pierced the invisible wall with a pleasing thrill. But this shrubbery was not really one of the great places of the garden; it was rather unresponsive and dull. I prefer, on leaving the white seat, to turn the corner of the curving wistaria-wall, which comes to an end just here, and pass into the formal enclosure behind it. The sun is quite high enough to beat freely into this sheltered retreat.

Face round, then, and turn the corner—but you see at once that the wall, which has come wandering up here from the wing of the house, does not really end at this point; it doubles sharply back on itself, enfolding a narrow space which entices my thought. The sprawling branches of a quince-tree appear over the wall, from within; but leave that for the present, remembering that the secret garden of the quince must be visited in due course. It is now the " Dutch garden " that calls—not very Dutch, in truth, but that was how we knew it. A broad oblong with a geometrical parterre, gravelled paths, box edgings, walled on three sides—it was Dutch enough for our fancy. The fourth side was shadowed by the cool shrubbery. And so I guide you to another white seat, tucked under the honeysuckle of one of the walls and overlooking the parterre; and this is a very celebrated corner, one of the most rewarding in all the garden. In these morning hours the children are constantly ranging in this neighbour-hood, with the seat for their headquarters, em-

bowered in honeysuckle and overhanging ivy-
bunches.

It was celebrated; there was an old story of one
of the Gurneys, of Aunt Fry in her maiden youth,
which centred about this seat. Our grandfather
liked to tell the story, pacing the gravelled path in
his long-skirted black coat and pointing out the
seat with his umbrella; he told the legend in a sly
voice, with a chuckle, dramatically pausing. It is
not much of a story, and I never really believed it;
but it was supposed that Aunt Fry, then Elizabeth
Gurney, had been wavering, delaying, demurring
under the discreet attentions of her suitor—he could
get no decided answer from her at all. So the
matter stood when he determined at length to offer
her a present, a valuable gift of a fine gold watch
and chain; and of course if she accepted it she
committed herself—a true young Quakeress does
not accept a gold watch from a man whom she
proposes to keep at a distance. But this was a very
discreet young man; he would not thrust the watch
in her face and confuse her bashfulness. Unobtrusively he laid it in her path—laid it on this very
seat under the wall, at which our grandfather points
with his baggy umbrella; for this way she would
pass, she would see the token, she would understand. So the young man steals to the seat,
deposits his offering and effaces himself. But what
happens when a man is courting one of seven
sisters? Of course the other six are on the tiptoe of
curiosity and their prying eyes are everywhere.
The six other Miss Gurneys, I tell you, were all on
the spot, hidden among the bushes, when Betsy

(they called her Betsy) came strolling past the seat, eyed the fatal gift and stood hesitating. She paused, she mused, she turned away. But her sisters knew their Betsy, you may be sure; they waited and watched; and I need scarcely say that the ridiculous girl was presently seen edging back towards the seat again, and she picked up the watch, and she took the young man Fry, and by every account she was a good wife to him—a good wife, but perhaps, if I may hint as much, a little less interested in her own hearth than in her prisoners and her admirable activities on their behalf. Well, it is long ago; and I never much believed in the story of the watch, as I said, though it was entertaining to listen to grandfather as he told it with twinkles and chuckles. Such was the fame of the, seat, however, and I would not decry it.

2

Enough of that; for us this region of the garden had better titles. Close against the seat was a small ivy-mantled tool-house; and further along, in an angle of the wall, there was a tiny round pond, with a fountain, where the motionless noses of frogs protruded among the draggle of slimy green weed; and beside it there was a green-house, full of damp and luscious fragrance; and then again there was a door that led to the secret close of the quince-tree, and all the mazes of attraction that lay in that quarter. How easy to be led on and on—but I tend to return to the legendary seat, partly because I should have collected a treasury there of odds and ends (you know how one accumulates a heap of things which it seems necessary to preserve, in the course of a morning), partly because I must take proper stock of this neighbourhood before wandering further. From the Dutch garden there was a charming view of the rambling roofs and chimneys of the house. You saw them sliced off, so to speak, by the line of the garden-wall, with its spray and foam of white clematis. The gables, the tiled slopes at odd angles, the beautiful chimneys in their ruffles of greenery, made a bewildering mass, a view like that of a little old red-roofed town, weather-stained to a soft richness of rose-red and tawny-brown. The outbuildings, the brew-house and the stables, ranged away to the right, with a yellower rust of lichen dappled over their ash-grey tiles; the great heads of the limes and chestnuts rose sumptuously behind them.

As for the queer collection of objects that by now I may have amassed in my corner, I could tell a story about each of them if I had the face to do so. But it is difficult to share with another the peculiar sense of their value—how it is that a mossed stone, one of a hundred, or a handful of duckweed squeezed out like a sponge, or a bunch of crisp and crackling "everlastings," may have appealed to one as striking and desirable, apt for possession. They are collected and bestowed with care—but not of these will I speak. There was a small covered basket, however, about three inches deep, of which something may be said, though it has been kept a secret hitherto. We had brought that basket from home, from far away, on the journey to Earlham, and nobody but the children knew what it contained.

IN THE GARDEN

A beetle, very large, black as ebony, with a little earth for it to burrow in on the way—it was a beetle that we had brought hither, intending to set it free in the garden at Earlham. And now was the moment; the beetle stepped forth upon alien ground, doubtfully paced and paused; and I cannot forget the incident, now that the crunch of the gravel and the dry smell of the box-borders is about me again, at ten o'clock of a fine summer morning. The beetle may finally have advanced along Wilberforce's Walk, which ran in a straight vista down the edge of the shrubbery in this quarter. Wilberforce perhaps, on just such a morning, once strolled there with Uncle Joseph John, plotting the holy war upon the slave-driver; the path was named after him. It was long and straight and shady; the two friends in their broad-brimmed hats could just have walked abreast; and you would have seen them pass out into sunshine at the far end, as they turned to follow the path which made the circuit of the lawn.

The day grew much hotter very soon; even the green pool in the corner of the Dutch garden had lost its chill, when I hung over the railing that surrounded its stone lip and plunged a hand into the clammy duckweed. Against the wall in that corner there was a splendid fig-tree; but we could afford to neglect the figs. There was better to come, and the way to it, if I choose to take the way, is immediately here. Hard by the pool there is a door in the brick wall; and dropping my lump of green ooze, which keeps the stamp of the fingers that squeezed it, I turn to grasp the smooth handle of the

door. Here, as ever, I am delayed by the pleasant
feel of the fluted and egg-shaped knob—the more so
that it works very stiffly, needing a powerful wrench.
Outside lay the paddock, and then the kitchen-
garden; and no doubt there comes a time, under
the towering noon-day, when there is an imperious
call in that direction. I don't know that the moment
has arrived just yet; but meanwhile it would be as
well to give a glance round the paddock. So the
door swings open, and shuts behind me with its
familiar thump.

3

Here was a change of scene. A rough track ran
along this outer face of the wall, heading for the
park, and the paddock was just over the way. It
was a small stretch of open grass, and principally
it was interesting on account of the ice-house, which
stood at one end of it. Stood?—it lay buried rather,
with the turf rolling over it in a hump, like a gigantic
grave. It was entered, or had been of old, by a low
door with wooden bars; but I suppose it had long
fallen out of use. I think we used to hear that it had
been the habit to hack great blocks of ice in winter
out of the frozen pond, down in the park, and store
them away in this kingly tomb; but somehow that
information never explained the place for me. An
ice-house, silent, glittering, steel-blue—a dazzling
thought! And nothing was to be seen but a grassy
mound and a low doorway, hinting at a vault full
of mouldering bones. Where, then, was the house
of ice? I never got that question straight in my

mind, and the note of perplexity still pervades this end of the paddock.

I do not follow the rough cart-road into the park; I face in the other direction, edging along in the shadow of the garden-wall. Further and further it ran, and at one point it bore on its breast a battered target, dimly painted with the form of an antlered stag. At times our uncles used to bang and blaze at the runnable stag from the paddock; but all is peaceful at this hour, and I can narrowly inspect the riddled form of the great beast. Still clinging to the wall I pass the entrance to the back-yard—that green common which I looked out upon, you may remember, while the gardener was arranging the flowers and the poor man from Norwich sat patient in his corner. I pass on, and now I am very near the gate of the kitchen-garden; but the cart-road avoids it, and presently plunges into the shadow of a grove of horse-chestnuts, to join the drive, the main approach to the front-door of the house. So I have skirted round the group of outbuildings, the suburbs of the house; and having once arrived among the horse-chestnuts I might not find it easy to get further for the moment. For if pebbles and chunks of moss and seed-pods and such things seem to cry out to be " collected," what about the delicious objects, brown and satin-smooth, that strew the ground under these trees? A chestnut, breaking out of its thorny husk in beautifully fitted segments —and best of all when it is unripe, creamily piebald —has a charm irresistible, no doubt; the trouble is only that they are too plentiful, scattered by the thousand, so that they want the lasting appeal of rarity. Let them lie, after all; the stables are near by, and there is an audible hissing and stamping and clanking that entices me thither.

The coachman was a very handsome man, fresh-coloured, curly-headed; I can describe him exactly by saying that he looked like one of those fine racy gentlemen, half squires, half farmers, who figure in the novels of George Eliot, of Mrs. Gaskell; there is more than one of them, I think, in Cranford alone. He bloomed and beamed upon the carriage-box; but properly he should always have driven a high dog-cart, spanking cheerily off to market and exchanging a seasonable pleasantry with every one on the road. That was his look, his type; but perhaps there was an indolent ease in his gesture which belied it, and I dare say Mrs. Gaskell's brisk north-country eye would have rejected him from her gallery. He and his underling seemed busy and active enough, however, as we drifted into the stable-yard to watch the grooming of the horses—that quaint old operation, unknown, I suppose, to many young observers to-day. It is not at all like the oleaginous smearing and dabbing of a motor-car, which turns the stable-hand into a grimy hybrid of a stoker and a rag-picker. Our friend and his under-ling were not dingily messing with oil-cans and dirty rags; they were stamping about in their thick clog-boots and sluicing their horses' legs with clean buckets of water, they were rubbing and hissing in an atmosphere of pungent freshness and coolness—how different from the " savour of poisonous brass and metal sick " that to-day hangs heavy and sluggish in the stable-yard! The coach-house, too, was a rare place, and the thin staleness of the air inside a shut carriage was not less agreeable in its way than the rich tang of the stalls and the loose-boxes.

The venerable pile of the stables included lofts, raftered spaces aromatic with apples, with hay, roof-cavities where shafts of powdered light fell slanting on the planked floors. It reminds one of a ship—would not a steep ladder, suddenly opening at your feet through a square hole in the boards, be what they call a " companion-way ? " There is deck upon deck ;—but on the whole I prefer the open air, and the green back-court, of which the stable-building forms one side. There the pump, the great pump under its cloister in the corner, would attract me first. Surely it was remarkable ; under the cloister-roof a beam revolved upon a central pillar, and there dangled from the beam a kind of collar, through which the horse's head was thrust. The collar was made fast ; and the horse tramped round and round the pillar, carrying the beam, you see, along with him. So the water was pumped into the house ; the mouth of the well was close by, under the kitchen window, and while the horse was at work you could hear that horrible noise of pulsing jangling water, far down in the blackness, which to some of us is so singularly unnerving. I disquiet myself without need, how-ever ; for at this hour the three slender rods that dive into the depth are still and silent ; it was long ago, in the very early morning, when I heard the measured thud of the pump in action. I have now no hesitation in screwing past the well-head to grasp the bars of the kitchen window. The head of Mrs. Chapman's handmaid appeared within, and I told her of the projected plan of a picnic on the river. "I 'ope you won't get drownded and all," she said pleasantly.

The rough grass of the court lifted gently away from the back-door. The stable-building to the left, of worn old flint and brick, was largely covered by an ancient pear-tree, trained against the wall; and under the rim of the eaves there was a sun-dial, on which I always tried to read the hour and never succeeded. That was one side of the court; on the other, to the right, there was a low line of red brick-work—and I am greatly surprised to find that I cannot account for the whole of it. The little chamber with the brick oven, where Mrs. Chapman baked the bread—that was there; but what else? It is the first blind spot that I have discovered in the insatiable eye of remembrance. I scan that low wall, which certainly had doors and windows in it—first a door that led to the enclosure of the quince, and then the bake-house. But there was more; and by some chance the blur of a mist descends in that quarter—odd and bitter it is to feel so helpless to dispel it. All is clear again, however, at the upper end of the green patch, and I march thither in full confidence.

There was here a curiosity. Against the bounding wall stood an aviary, a space of wirework with a small wooden hut on either side; and within this cage were two great glowering birds—eagles. A pair of golden eagles had been acquired, I don't know where or how, by one of our uncles; and here

in our time they were living out their old age.
Charles and Maria—they stared mutely, with fixed
and sinister eyes. Their look was hostile and
revengeful; it was our theory that to venture into
their cage would mean instant death—to any one,
that is, but our remarkable friend the butler, who
flung open the cage-door, strode in and patted them
familiarly on their humped backs. I don't think
they soared and chafed in spirit, I think their
minds were set on the lumps and gobbets of nameless flesh that were brought them by our friend; but
when one of them, after fixing us with a yellow
unwinking gaze, suddenly lurched and shouldered
off his perch and flopped towards the side of the
cage, it was always an effort to hold firm and affront
him without giving way, even with the wire between
us. There came at length a day when we found,
returning to Earlham, that the aviary had vanished.
Charles and Maria were dead and stuffed; they had
gone indoors to join the fascinating company upon
the landing of the staircase, with the herons and
the ruffs. I should like to watch them humping
their backs for Sidell to scratch them again.

And next to the cage of the eagles, against the
same wall, was the fives'-court, and the patter of the
balls was to be heard there at times. It was a court
of archaic design, and the grass grew freely between
the flags; but I certainly hear the noise of the balls
and the scuffling of feet, while I stray in this region.
You could not very well look on at the game,
however, for it was a court enclosed upon all four
sides, with a small entrance-gate at one corner;
there was no proper view to be had of the young men

at their game, as they leaped and scuffled, calling
the score in sharp monosyllables. I should pass on,
therefore, and issue out once more into the quarter
of the paddock, plainly veering this time towards
the gate of the kitchen-garden.

4

A high wooden gate, painted white—my hand is
on the latch, and it sticks and jams for a moment.
Once within the gate I should turn, beyond question,
to the right. A few yards of cindery path, and then
the floor is firm and smooth under my feet, and I am
in the shade of a wonderful old tree. It is a tree
of great limbs, heavy with age; its failing arms are
propped here and there upon stout crutches. But
its leafage is thick and abundant; and lurking
among the leaves, or better still, strewing the bare
floor, here are the mulberries in their hundreds.
To a few of us it is revealed that the mulberry is
paragon and nonsuch among the fruits of the
garden; it is what all the rest of them would be if
they could. And surely the path that advances
towards a mulberry-tree on a morning of late
summer, that lingers about the ample trunk and
spreads a clean cool surface beneath its shade—
that is the path to follow, now and ever. There is
this about mulberries, that you can only attain to
them on their own ground; you must go to them,
search them out where they lie; they are too
precious and tender, with their bursting purple
juices, to be handled and transported to meet you.
A ripe black mulberry is a gift to you direct from
the opulent tree; and I cannot help it if I pass on

my way, after an interval, plentifully stained with noble dyes.

Just beyond the mulberry-tree you come to the region of the hot-houses. And beware!—for peering in at the door of the earth-cool potting-shed, I caught sight of the gardener, and I own I was chilled by his eye. He was a hard man, I always thought—angular, light-eyed, with a wisp of fox-red beard; his glance was quelling, it was like a thin whistle of wind in the golden calm of the kitchen garden. We could not feel at ease in this saturnine presence, not though now and again, as I remember, he would silently lead us to the peach-house or the vinery and offer us each a selected portion. I expect we did him an injustice, and I perfectly see that he had good reason to lock those hot-houses and pocket the key; but the sun shone warmer when he turned, still without a word, and marched away to the white gate. The other good souls, who were digging among the cabbages or skilfully tapping the plants out of their pots in the cool shed—they were all friendliness; and especially I am glad to loiter and stare where old Gayford bends over his spade. For how many years, I wonder, had he been digging the borders and banking the celery-beds at Earlham? The sing-song drawl of his Norfolk speech echoes tunefully from a far distance.

And now for the orchid-houses, here at hand, of which I seem able to number several. Our grand-father was a studious collector and cultivator of orchids; and surely that was an exotic amusement which fitted oddly with his home-grown piety and simplicity. Some queer monstrosity of a cattleya or an odontoglossum always stood in a tiny glass on his writing-table, cheek by jowl with a Gloire de Dijon or a Maréchal Niel; it did not strike him that the orchid had an impious look beside the rose. These houses in the kitchen-garden were full of fantastic outlandish creatures, dangling and writhing in vaporous heat; and his black coat, his clerical white tie, his stout umbrella, appear incongruously to me now, among that luxuriance of streaked and slashed and maculated colour, more flesh than flower. It was suitable that he should fondle his roses in the open air; but indeed his love of flowers was not sentimental, not that of the mild old clergyman indulging a hobby—it was grave and scholarly. I think of him as glancing at the rose with secret warmth, but as speaking of it only to name the species with a quiet interest; and the same tone would serve in the orchid-house, when he guided us among the steaming tiers of the stove-plants. He was scientific, he was slightly distant with his flowers of whatever complexion; so that his association with these shameless languorous aliens was not compromising. They were certainly magnificent; we gaped in wonder, and enjoyed the stifling vapour-bath of the tropical forest.

But that is an interlude; I am soon out of doors and at home again, where the bordered walk runs down the middle of the kitchen-garden. Such a tall pale hollyhock (with its " talking eyes," as Browning said of another who was tall and pale) stands at my right hand—tall and gracious, lemon-pale, towering up to the laden apple-bough that leans over the path. Apples of gold, a kind of cowslip gold, clear and unflushed, were heaped in great drifts upon the trees which shadowed that walk; rose-red apples too, well burnished, shone in their darker and crisper leafage. The path ran straight ahead, dappled and barred with sunlight, to the southern fruit-wall at the end. There I see a covered seat against the wall, a recess enarched with clematis and honeysuckle; and the seat is occupied by the bee-hive, to which the bees come swinging down from their voyages in all quarters. Now turn to the right, along the face of the wall, and stop just where I tell you, after twenty yards or so. These are plums indeed—there are none better in the garden. They grow on the wall at this point and nowhere else, these particular plums; the round sort, almost as big as peaches, with that wonderful blue powder-bloom. And then to the right again; and there is the vast netted enclosure of the currants and the gooseberries. It is easy to filch open the door of that great cage; but really I think I could pass it by just now, after all that has happened already. In the height of the noonday the kitchen-garden seems suddenly to become one broad blaze, and I could wish to find myself picked up in a moment and carried elsewhere. It is an endless journey back to the white gate in the corner.

5

It was pleasant to reach the thick shade of the chestnuts in the drive again, where it sidled towards the north front of the house. I think I have said that the house on this side was bare and buff-white with plaster, a great contrast to the vines and roses and red brick of the face towards the garden. Here, to the north, two wings of the house reached out, enfolding a sweep of loose gravel; so that the carriage, as it wheeled round to the steps of the front-door, entered a small echoing court-yard—you might call it a court-yard, though the fourth side was open. If I should take my stand on the semi-circle of the steps I should look straight down the lime-avenue and the drive that runs out there to the church and the village; the other approach, by way of the chestnuts, turns in from the right, and that is the direction of Norwich, the Norwich road of arrival and departure.

These steps of the front-door delay me unexpectedly; they are more interesting than I had remembered. The door itself, in the first place, and the big knocker, and the pediment over the door—and then on either side, under the wall of the house, iron-barred gratings in the gravelled floor, and brick cavities beneath them, fringed with ferns—and what is more, all the windows of the wing to the left are sham and blank, a peculiarity that takes my fancy; and a good many minutes have flown while I review these points in order, not forgetting to count the sham windows with care, six in all, two in each storey. On that wall, moreover, is the bell-handle which the coachman seizes as we drive up to the door. How long, how long could I be occupied in these blest meditations? I have nothing to show for them but a collection of facts, tiny facts of a knocker and a grating, a cornice, the wire of a bell, amassed and assorted and

arranged till they lie in their receptacle like the bits
of a puzzle. Only when each is neatly in its place,
only when I am secure in possession of them all,
am I ready to leave them and pass on. No scholar,
no laborious and disinterested pedant, hangs more
lovingly than a child over a fact, a mere fact as such.
I neither criticize nor reflect; from the creamy
texture of the plaster to the toad among the ferns,
everything that I add to my collection has an equal
value, is inserted in its place with the same intent
concentration of care. I could really feel impatient
at the thought of that unremitting gaze, bovine
positively, which refuses to be crossed or disturbed.
What could the child be about, loitering there upon
the door-steps in a vacant dream? But that is
unreasonable; I enjoy my hoard of facts at this
late hour, and I owe them all to the slow stare of the
child.

So much for that. Now I should wish to turn the
corner of the blind-eyed wing, and pass through the
small iron gate in the railing there. This is a side-
way into the garden, and first I find myself in the
narrow grassy dell of the weeping ash. It is clear,
therefore, that the bow-window of the ante-room,
with its view of the ash, projects at this end of this
wing of the house. It does; and the mossy green
dell runs away alongside of the lime avenue. A
narrow strip of mown grass, spongy with moss, set
with a few flower-beds—I think of it as a dell
because it lies like a trough between the great
breezy limes on this side and a shrubbery of oaks
on that. The grass is like the deepest plush to
walk on, for it is a very shady recess, and the roots

of the moss are always damp. The weeping boughs
of the ash drop almost to the ground; you may
push them aside like a curtain, letting them fall
behind you; and so thickly they are woven, it is
certainly as good as a bell-tent. This oak-shrubbery
here, I may say, is perhaps the best in the garden;
it lies on uneven ground, and under the trees is a
scrub of bushes, with here and there a gravelly
break or clearing, and there is a bank which is
covered with those strange paper seed-heads of the
plant called honesty; and it is a wood that is always,
always tuneful with the crooning of pigeons, so
much so that never once have I heard the coo of a
wood-pigeon in a tree without instantly flashing
away to the oaks at Earlham, to tread the spongy
grass again and thrust in among the rustling stalks
of the honesty. And then a step or two takes me
out of the wood and on to the west lawn.

Yes, I reach the west lawn, where the view opens
out over the park and down to the river. This lawn
is not a great plain, like the other. It is small;
half a minute will bring me to the drop of the sunk
fence on the further side. That is our way to the
river and the boat-house; the heronry is down
there, and the rookery and the water-meadows
beyond it. But all that is not for this morning, and
there is still plenty of ruminant adventure laid up
in the precinct of the garden, without going further
afield. I have reached the west lawn, and still I
have not touched the wilderness of long grass where
the rain-gauge is, and the mossy path that encircles
it, and the laurels and the " sulky-walk " (why
sulky?—you would never guess; but wait). A

mazy paradise still lies ahead, before I shall have completed the circuit of the garden. And even as I stand wavering, doubtful which delight to follow next, the bell rings out from the distant belfry of the kitchen, and the endless morning has come to an end. Luncheon!—the bell was a signal that it was time to go in and get your face washed. Our grandmother, perhaps, was strolling in the sulky-walk, enjoying the shadow. " Well, dear children, have you had a nice long morning in the garden ? " A timeless morning it had seemed, till this moment ; and now it was suddenly finished, caught in the flying hours. As I entered the garden-door my mulberry-dyes did not escape the notice of an uncle, who was lounging loosely and mightily in the porch.

6

An hour later the whole company was gathered in a shady spot, somewhere on the edge of the great lawn, sociably relaxed. And here is a historic note. One of the young men was describing, I remember, a new-fashioned game, introduced from elsewhere, that he had lately seen played, had played himself ; and I listened to his account with curiosity. The game was played over wide spaces of country, with a smiting of balls that had to be driven from point to point. There were marked stages in the course to be followed, and you had to drive your own little ball through each of them, your object being to outdo your opponent—in speed, as I understood, not very clearly following the explanation in this matter. A vision of two men racing over bare hills, brandishing some form of croquet-mallet against the sky as they sped—a vision all mingled with the dapple of sunlight under the oak-tree, and the softness of the brown rug on which I lay stretched, and the green purity of the acorns with which I was playing—this picture, this complexity of sensation, assumed a name, as our uncle developed his tale, which had the sound of " goff." Historic indeed; not one of the party had ever seen the game, except this uncle, and there was something wild and grand about my picture that later history has signally failed to fulfil.

The question of the " goff " was debated languidly; it was a prime hot afternoon. Grandfather had changed his long black coat for a long grey one, thin like paper; and over my acorns I had an ear for his story of its purchase. He had seen it in a shop-window on his travels, had asked the price. Fifteen shillings—" Then done widge you! " cried grandfather; I delighted in the humorous bucolic turns (if that is what they were) of his talk. But as usual he was only beaming and pausing on the edge of the group. He soon tramped off to his study; and I suppose the rest of the party drifted and scattered, for certainly before long the children were being " read to," while they were held to their repose on the brown rug. I forget the reading —or rather I could easily remember it if I chose, but I prefer to let it sing in my ears as a tune without words, drowsily lulling. Perhaps it was a chapter of our peerless Dickens—or was it only an artless anecdote of a pair of children who roamed and played in a beautiful old garden? I must think that our taste was readily satisfied. A story is a story, and if it has plenty of detail, the minuter the better, so that you can see for yourself what is happening in it, I confess it matters little to me whether it is a story of Dickens or a story of Louisa Alcott. It is definition, precision that we want, no cloudy fancies. Whether it is Great Expectations or Harry and Laura, The Rose and the Ring or Little Men, our cry is equally punctual when the last page is turned. " Now begin it again "—after living so deeply into the company of a book one does not easily forsake it for another, to make the acquaintance of a set of strangers. Yet there are chords, too, in the soul which sometimes thrill with a different rapture, different in kind. The delight of a story is one thing, and I love it well; I transfer the story into my life, and live on it, feed on it, in pleasant tracts of rumination. But there is also the thrill of the sound of words, so piercing, so rending that it is hardly to be called a pleasure, though for the moment all the world is worthless in comparison with it. I might hear the sound, perhaps, in this drowsy hour under the oak-tree— you never know.

From our corner of the lawn, as I lay in the shade, I could look aslant at the many-windowed breadth of the house, over a foreground of marigolds and verbenas. The sun was slanting too, by this time; it no longer stared full in the face of the house, it was creeping towards the west, throwing the angle of the dining-room into shadow and revealing the depths of its green mantling, blue-green streamers and plumes of jessamine starred with white. The wing of the dining-room flanked the deep border that stretched before the house, interrupted only by the porch of the central door—a loosely crowded border in which heliotrope, moss-roses, great bushes of geranium, were massed to the window-sills of the ground-floor. At the further end another low wing stood forward; and here the sun was now beginning to strike the ample spread of an apricot-tree on the wall, a tree that was placed to receive the steady goodness of the afternoon blaze. I could count the apricots that were mellowing there in the distance, for they were all tied up in their little white hoods of muslin, to guard them from the wasps. Rich and deep was the day, gathering its power, bending its great energy to ripen the teeming garden. And then, I dare say, across the dreamy contentment of the hour, there might suddenly reach me the sound of the words—the words that have been nothing hitherto but the telling of a story, the unregarded instrument which a story has used.

A handful of them escape from the rest, darting up like living creatures. I scarcely consider their sense; it is their life, their wheeling curve and cut through the air, their poise, their fall—it is their bird-free movement that is entrancing. They were simply a phrase in a book—a poetry-book, as it chanced; but they soared out of the book in an instant and caught me after them. They wheel and sing, and I have no attention for anything else, not even for the story or the poem out of which they have shot. Well, I forget the rest; it matters little what it was all about. The living words, in their magic of freedom and beauty, have nothing

to do with the interest and the charm of a story;
they are as a flash from another world, pure and
absolute, a stroke of art. And what were they?
I shall keep them to myself, for in fact they were
poor poetry. But they were words, and they cast
the enchantment of words into the mind of one
listener at any rate, while the sun rounded the
corner of the house and blazed upon the hooded
apricots.

7

A tall figure came tip-toeing with elaborate precautions, with warning gestures, towards our settlement under the oak-tree. This was the tallest and
mightiest of our uncles, the soldier-uncle; he
advanced with signals of dismay, beckoning to the
elders of our party and trumpeting a deep stage-
whisper through his hands. "Callers!" He
seemed shocked by the news he brought. He strode
up to our cousin, who was sitting near at hand, and
clutched her wildly. "Callers!" It was very
dramatic, as though some blow unforeseen had
suddenly fallen upon a peaceful family, shattering
their security. A carriage of callers had been
sighted, strangers were at the gate—what was to be
done about it? Flight was the word; and the
garden, so much of it as could be seen from the
house, was quickly depopulated. Whoever had
been enjoying the deepening shade, on our side of
the lawn, melted and was gone. With the zest of
conspirators we retreated stealthily down the green
alley of the sulky-walk.

The sulkies stood at the far end of it. They were

a pair of white seats, one on either side of the walk—
covered seats, like rounded sentry-boxes, with
shallow conical roofs to them; at a distance they
looked like great white barrels with peaked lids.
They swung round upon pivots, facing to the sun
or the shade as you might choose. Both occupants
would presumably wish for the same aspect; and
so, if you think it out, you will see that they would
never face towards each other—and hence the name.
The sulkies were very old; they had stood at the
end of that green walk in the time of the seven Miss
Gurneys, and a hundred years later they turned
stiffly and shakily upon their pivots. The narrow
bench inside the round barrel made a comfortless
perch, and nobody sat in them but the children,
who were drawn to the sulkies by their unlikeliness,
their singularity. I should naturally pause to seat
myself in one of them, and to note how the sides
of the barrel enclosed me, shutting off the world
except in one quarter. It made a little house, a
little fortress; I sat there for ten seconds perhaps,
just long enough to taste the sensation. Then I
slid off the bench, and followed the gravel path
which crossed this end of the green alley.

The gravel path ran round the whole outer circuit
of the garden, with the sunk fence and the park
immediately beyond it. But it was a very eventful
path, changing its character many times in its
course, disappearing from view behind the deep
shrubberies, re-emerging on the confines of the
open lawns. In the neighbourhood of the sulkies
it was secluded and bowery; trees over-arched it,
and in this region the sunk fence became a tangle,

a loose thicket of holly and oak. The gravel itself
was greened over with slippery films of mossiness;
and I particularly like the thought of a remarkable
tree, I think an ash, which I come upon almost
at once. It grew at the edge of the path, and it
had a twisted old trunk that sloped and lurched and
divided, and you could walk up it as by a flight
of steps. I have spent a whole afternoon between
the sulkies and this ash-trunk, amassing a new
collection of objects that invited the hand and the
eye—storing them away in the fortress of one of the
white seats, transferring them to the cool lichen
in the steps of the tree. Surely these children are
clever at devising their own amusements, or they
are easily amused. Some of our elders, strolling
by, might glance indulgently at our occupation;
it seemed to consist in shovelling together a litter
of pebbles and mosses, and ramming them into the
chinks of the tree. Is that a game to absorb a pair
of intelligent children and keep them busy as
beavers for a whole afternoon? All I can say is
that to me it appeared to call for both thought and
skill; but it was difficult to explain.

I prefer just now, however, to push ahead and to
follow the path in its circuit. Presently it left the
rustling shadows and came out into the great even
light of the big lawn; and there, away in the
distance, were the many windows of the house, the
long red roofs, the chimneys that were beginning to
catch a deeper gold from the westering sun—and
behind and above them the huge quiet domes of
lime and chestnut. The path marches forward
in a straight reach, always in view of the far-away

windows across the lawn; it marches along the
edge of the dry ditch, now broad and open, where
the fence of the park is concealed. And remark
that the slope of the ditch, next to the path, has
become an enormous flower-bed, tilted to the south
across the whole breadth of the lawn; a flower-bed
entirely given up to those beautiful old anemones,
purple and white and scarlet, with their crimped
ruffs of greenery on their clean stalks; and even
in this late summer there are always a few to be
seen, gleaming and flaming here and there upon the
brown earth and the faded leafage. I follow the
straight path, flooded with the sense of the lawn
and the open light and the benevolent gaze of the
house with its wide arms in the distance; I follow
the path—and once more it passes into shadow,
and the view of the house is cut off by a thicket
of trees and bushes. And very soon comes a sharp
turn; there is a gate into the park at the corner,
and with your back to the gate you look down the
narrow vista of a walk, densely shaded, screened on
either hand. It is Wilberforce's Walk, along which
I looked from the other end this morning.

Let me make the return journey, therefore, with
Wilberforce and Uncle Joseph John, while they still
wag their fine old heads together over their high
designs. But to tell the truth I did not give them
a thought, though I liked the notion that the walk
had a name, a title for its clear identity. There is
great virtue in a name, and it was a pity that the
garden on the whole was poor in this matter. The
alleys and dells and enclosures were all very personal
to us, very distinct in their tone and temper; and

128

to leave them nameless, as most of them were left, was a slight from which they suffered. The thicket of the oaks and the honesty and the wood-pigeons, for example, was an intimate companion whose engaging moods I knew by heart; but his want of a proper name, in which they would all be summed up, made it impossible to allude to him familiarly, to circulate him in talk, to call to him in absence with an easy quick nod of recognition. Our fancy, I note with surprise, did not soar to the creation of new names; but new names, I think, would have seemed artificial, unnatural. I felt the difference when I came to Wilberforce's Walk; there was somebody one could mention at any time, and all would understand the allusion.

Here I am, then, once more in the walled garden of Betsy's seat, the box-edged parterre and the frog-pond. But it is a scene completely changed from this morning. Where there was winking stirring sunshine, where there was shadow cold and crisp from the touch of night, there is now a grey softness in the shadow, and the sunshine is a flood of gold as still as glass. Especially under the wall where the clematis foams in its white cascade there is shadow that has already the purity of twilight, though there are hours and hours of full daytime still to come. I always like the nasturtiums that riot along the foot of this wall, bright yellow, bright red; very few plants of the earth are as clean in negligent ease as a yellow nasturtium. And then there are the great stalks of the giant balsam, holding out the ripe pods, full charged, that explode with a snap and a splutter as I touch them off. But it is a doorway in the wall, at the further end of it, that I aim for at present—the door of the quince-tree close, where I have not penetrated yet. That would be the right retreat for whatever may be left of the afternoon.

It was a narrow strip, or rather a long and tapering angle, between two high walls. At the broader end there was an approach from the kitchen; it must have been the herb-garden in old days. The quince-tree was very ancient and fruitful, but I am not deceived by the luminous beauty of the quinces; they look so mild, so mellow, and in point of fact you might as well try to gnaw a stone off the road. As for the kitchen-herbs, I think there was still some growth of sage and mint and such things in this quarter; but the place had been dedicated, long before our time, to the children of the house, for their own private planting and gardening. Their traces had vanished, the secluded corner was untended; yet the later children felt they possessed a lien, a claim that might be asserted, perhaps, on some spare afternoon when it seemed convenient to plant and dig, and particularly to water. These operations are interesting, and best of all is the care of reviving the new plants, limp and gasping from the trowel, with copious showers; the process is apt to end in a tropical deluge, the garden lapses into a slobbering mud-pie. And indeed I know very well where the trowel and watering-pot are to be found. There is a tool-house not far off, full of seductive implements; seedlings of marigold and stock are soon lifted from a neighbouring border; and I dare say there is plenty of time to reach the period of the mud-pie before we are called indoors. Clean crumbling earth is good, but juicy and all-pervading slime is better; it spreads with wonderful rapidity, from the skirts of the clothing to the very roots of the hair. And when somebody arrives to hale us indoors at tea-time, somebody throws up her hands with shrill cries at our bedabblement.

8

That scare of callers had long since blown over; but when we emerged again on to the lawn after tea, cleaned and refreshed, it was likely that we might find the family party augmented. In these summer weeks the arms of Earlham were very wide, and there was much coming and going of its large and faithful flock. Moreover for many miles around the land was colonized by the children and grand-children, the cousins in every degree, of the sons of Earlham; in many and many villages of the country-side its kinsmen dwelt and increased. A stranger would be bewildered by the intricate system of relationship that spread over half the county and knitted it with Earlham; cross-ties, intermarriages, confused the web beyond unravel-ling by any but those who were born to it. I could almost say that if, starting from Earlham, you should tack to and fro in a certain line from village to village, you might travel for a week and never pass a square flint church-tower that does not shadow some kindred settlement, some shoot from the stock of the old Norwich Friends. Norfolk is a land of " halls "; wherever you go you find that the main house of the village, modest or grandiose, is still as it was in the beginning, the hall; and sometimes the "old hall," a rambling group of gables and chimneys down by the river, has survived when the "new hall," in the modern taste, has arisen hard by on higher ground. I could not count all the Norfolk halls, new and old, that were of the kith of Earlham; but their village-names were very familiar to us, and they were united by a notable bond. The tie of blood was greatly respected, always in that English manner that mixes so much independence with its fealty. We were clansmen—that we distinctly felt; but the pieties and loyalties of an English family are mercifully untheoretic, and I suppose they were never yet allowed to become an inconvenience. Of a tough old "family-feeling," however, fast and loose, scrupulous and casual, let those speak who may view it from without—sometimes with impatience, I quite believe.

"Dear So-and-so is very faithful," our grandmother would say, and there was much meaning in the word. Dear So-and-so, perhaps, may have driven over this afternoon, bringing a gift of fidelity to the associations of Earlham which grandmother appreciated keenly, not less so than the tribute of personal affection to herself. When we reached the lawn after our nursery-tea, we should find the party of our elders gathered once more in the spreading shade; and I see that we approach rather shyly and doubtfully, on discovering the presence of a new-comer. What a curse that shyness can be, that well-known effluence that suddenly descends to tie the tongue and to cramp every joint of the body. Yet it does not stifle a movement of pleased curiosity, for otherwise I should turn at the garden-door and escape in another direction. That would be simple; but if there is company on the lawn I definitely wish to be there, I would not miss the entertainment of a new face, a new voice, an unfamiliar representation of some sort. And accordingly the approach must be faced—jauntily, shall it be, with an assumption of ease, or very cautiously, with as much self-effacement as possible? Either way I shall have chosen wrong, you will note; the demon of awkwardness sees to that. Jauntiness makes one flush to remember afterwards, self-effacement is even more conspicuous. But once among the party, when I hang upon the chair of a trusted ally, then I must say that I find the show rewarding. Dear So-and-so would hardly suspect what devouring eyes, what attentive ears, are following the details of her little performance.

Do not imagine, however, that it is a pair of ill-mannered children, or precociously critical, who have joined the circle on the lawn. Our kindly relatives, from those whom we knew well to the dim outlying ranges of the cousinhood where discrimination failed—they were watched, I will say, with discretion and in all simplicity. The faithful So-and-so was not one, but many, and each received the meed of our tongue-tied attention. The talk might be supposed to have no interest for the children; but nothing came amiss to them, I think, and I have listened with satisfaction, often enough, while two of our elders made talk with each other that had certainly no interest for themselves. And then, too, an arrival of some of the cousinhood brought an infusion into the air of intercourse that I recognized, though I could not have said what it was. A waft of life as it is lived in a country province, something that set the imagination vaguely circulating among bowery lanes and blue turnip-fields and sluggish waters, where small shabby villages straggle about the ornate grey churches of more spacious days—something from the very heart of that East Anglian ancientry came poetically stirring and breathing into our midst. These children were used to another landscape, one that spoke poetically too, but in quite a different idiom. At Earlham a world was revealed that lay apart, sufficient to itself, following its own ways and talking its own language—or no, not revealed indeed, but hinted at, implied and assumed, in the friendly incursions of the neighbourhood. I remember the obscure impression of distances that opened, with momentary glimpses of a life where the round of the year revolved and revolved in an unknown system, out there among the beautiful old village-names of the east country.

So Earlham was a liberal education, it is evident, at all hours of the day; here am I receiving after tea, most unconsciously, a lesson in the moral and social geography of our packed little island. And I don't know that anything counted for more in it than the appealing romance of the Norfolk names, which stole into the mind and coiled about the fancy with their clear and liquid syllables. Words like Hindringham, Walsingham, Burlingham, fell with a strain of rippling melody that echoed out of serene sky-spaces, shining reedy meres—if only it were possible to waylay these haunting intimations in plain prose. I never forget the little shock of delight with which I once heard our grandmother casually mention a name in which this clean euphony is roused to positive excitement. Here it is—Wramplingham!—and to say all, I think it a name that should be set to music by Schubert. And then in another vein there is the erratic host of names that in speech have slipped the anchorage of their spelling—Wymondham, Happisburgh, Costessey, Poringland—names that we utter with a bland indifference (full of distinction, I felt) to the laws of the alphabet. If you pronounce them as they are spelt, I regard you with a glance of superiority, infinitely provoking. Merely to say " Hazeborough," to say " Cossey "—let these suffice—gives me a fine sense of community with an ancient province, the kingdom of the easterlings.

9

Or it may be that the accession to our party was of another sort entirely. Some time ago I dropped a word of the missionary to whom our grandfather had lent his disused rectory-house at Colney—a charming old house, with a magnolia among its sunny windows. It was constantly lent to some missionary or other, for his holiday-weeks in England; he brought his wife there, and his little daughter from school, and they dropped into an interlude of parochial home-life that was all ready made for them, you may say, by our grandparents'

care. The good man, for a few weeks he could think
he was a village-parson at home, with his roses and
his fat old pony and his little babbling daughter
whom he had not seen for so long. He had to leave
her behind at school, when he and his wife returned
to Uganda; but meanwhile they could imagine
that they were a home-keeping family in a parsonage of their own, except that at Colney there was
no responsibility, no need to be busier about the
parish than they chose. But to be sure they were
not idle; the good man delighted to join our grandfather in his pastoral round, to lend a hand in the
service on Sunday, and I dare say his wife might
volunteer at the harmonium, if the regular per-
former was on his holiday. They came from
Uganda, from India, from China; they came again,
and not a few of them grew to be familiar friends of
Earlham in course of years. It is quite likely that
the missionary of the moment and his wife may have
dropped in to tea this evening.

Our grandfather was profoundly learned in the
lore of the mission-field; nothing was deeper in his
mind than the thought of the many faithful sickles
that were putting in at all times to that harvest.
The good reaper who was among us this evening
had faced I know not what—hardship, disappointment, danger in the heart of darkness; but he did
not dwell on these, he told us of his encouragement
and reward, the friends and brothers whom he had
found among the uttermost tribes. I have a vision
of Sunday morning in Uganda, the log-hut of a
church, the rows of strange dark faces fervently
upturned, our friend in his white English surplice,

his wife at her harmonium. It was she who accompanied the rolling hymns; I know it, because it so happened that the children had visited her at Colney rectory one morning, and had seen the very instrument that was to travel with her into the wild. A little portable thing, scarcely more than a pair of bellows and a key-board—she showed it to us with pride. Her husband had gone up to London the day before, and her last direction to him had been to bring her some " violet-powder " that she needed; and he had returned with an odd-shaped case, about twice the size of a coal-scuttle. " Your violet-powder, my dear," said he; and behold it was a new harmonium, just what they wanted in Uganda, which he had brought her as a surprise. Is that a story worth telling, after thirty years and more? It seemed to me an excellent one; and indeed it seems so still, at this moment when it re-emerges after very many years of oblivion.

I think it a good story, because it strikes a particular note so firmly. Draw from it my sense of the unvarying humour of the English parsonage, the happy faculty of bright simplicity and domesticity that will never have been blighted, I take it, by all the hosts of heathendom upon the globe. Our friends had seen a great deal of a barbaric and I dare say a formidable world; they had gone out into the wilderness, they had striven with the dark unknown, they had raised their prayer and hymn under alien skies; and they came back to the rose-hung porch and the buttercup meadow, the trim lawn and the thrush in the lilac, with exactly the gush of cheerful piety, the native wood-note of

clerical mirth, which they had carried with them
upon their far adventure. That jest of the violet-
powder and the harmonium has been heard, do not
doubt it, on coral strands and in equatorial jungles.
Immutable, invincible, the genius of the sunny
parsonage makes its way to the ends of all the
earth. Wherever it touches, there it brings the
echoes and the savours of a Sunday evening at
home; shut your eyes when you hear the tinkle
of the church-bell in Borrioboola, and your feet
will carry you along the winding hedge-row, over
the stile and across the village-green. And now
that our friends are at Earlham again, seated about
the tea-table on the lawn, I look in vain for a trace
of the Borrioboolan climate upon the homely bloom
of their imagination. The honest lady, shining
with motherly kindness, tells the children a story
of black babies, green parrots, droll monkeys—I
forget how it ran; her husband, lean and strong,
speaks enthusiastically of his coloured flock, pointing his account with anecdotes of their zeal and
faith. But it is only their matter that is exotic;
their spirit is domestic as the buttercups of the
glebe.

Beyond these friendly folk, therefore, I had no
impression of a new world disclosed. I felt I had
nothing to learn about Sunday evening and the
church-bell and the singing of hymns; there were
no strange horizons to open in that quarter. And
somehow the tale of the babies and the monkeys
(if I have the theme aright—it is all a blur) failed
to strike home; the tale of the violet-powder and
the odd packing-case was apparently more sug-

gestive. But the fact of the missionary and his wife, their presence, their recurrence, is distinctly to be recognized in the memory of Earlham, and I could not wander there for long without coming upon their trace. I see our grandmother constantly devising some plan to help or solace or nourish them; I hear our grandfather quietly and proudly enumerating the details of their success in the field; the "Church Missionary Society," its fame, its history, its literature, is never very far from the scene. And I remember an incident that much impressed me with the depth and seriousness of our grandparents' interest in these questions. It was in Earlham church, one evening, and the twilit service was just over, and I was following our grandmother down the aisle; it was a day when there was a collection for foreign missions, and somebody stood by the door with a plate. Grandmother held her contribution in readiness, and I saw it. There were several of them in her hand, several indeed, and as we approached the door she suddenly passed one of them to me, that I might make an offering of my own. For a moment it lay in my hand, the first I ever felt there—a golden sovereign. I dropped it into the plate, awed by the greatness of the issue, the outpouring of treasure, the prodigal magnificence of the transaction.

10

At this hour the party will tend to scatter freely over the lawn, for now the sun is well in the west, and almost the whole of the great plain is grey and pale in shadow; only here and there, through a rift in the trees, a rich bar of gold still kindles the grass. To the furthest verge of the clear expanse I can stray reflectively, and never take a step without waking some keen small memory, some tiny glimpse of life that opens like a picture in its place. In many of them there is nothing, one would say, to make a picture at all, nothing to distinguish the particular moment from a thousand others; but when a chance attitude, a group, a lightly thrown word or two, has endured indestructibly for so long, I cannot help prizing it and lingering over it as though it were a marvel. Two young men in white flannels who are bracing and tightening a lawn-tennis net; a middle-aged lady who advances graciously, arching her long neck, her hands folded upon her stomacher; a languid gentleman, strolling and smiling, who has come with a party of neighbours and whom I somehow understand to be a bad character: such are my pictures, there are scores of them about as remarkable as these. And by virtue, I suppose, of that troublesome duality of which I have spoken, in some of them I see myself, a figure among the rest, taking the light like an object; as here by a border of flowers, close to the dining-room windows, where I shuffle and blink in the sun beside our cousin—and I look on at that striking episode from an independent point of view, perfectly detached.

Well, I cannot pass over the scene that springs into existence by a certain bench on the lawn, a white seat protected by a folding lid—thrown back at this moment, for the seat is occupied by two figures in converse. One of them is our grand-

mother, the other a rather unyielding and estranging
old lady, an aged relative upon a visit to Earlham.
In point of fact she was indulgently inclined to the
children; and the dear solicitude of our cousin,
who happens to be in charge of us, is exercised to
make us behave to her becomingly. Aunt Ellen
should have no reason to think us unpleasing,
unmannerly; it was a task that Mary had set
herself, she intended to see it through. But what a
task—you would understand her difficulty if you
saw the hunched shoulders, the obstinate backs of
the children, whenever she tries to steer them
surreptitiously in the direction of Aunt Ellen; for
indeed the old lady was forbidding in her style, and
I cannot pretend that there was a high polish upon
that of the children. Mary, however, was ingenious;
she laid her plan, she invented a game; and as we
skirmished round her on the lawn, at a good distance from Aunt Ellen, she swiftly delivered her
stroke. " Run, run to that seat over there! "—
it was the climax of the game, and the game would
be won by the first to reach the seat. It was
decidedly thin; but Mary was so quick and brilliant
that she could always convince you, always impose
a dramatic artifice of that kind. Aunt Ellen had
the moving spectacle of a pair of children who
rushed across the lawn to her with cries and bleats,
overpowered (she thought) by the desire to greet
and welcome her. We had a great success.

So the next day she travelled off to Norwich,
announcing to Mary her intention to buy us each
a little present. And we were not to be trusted;
Mary knew these children, and knew that it was not

safe to leave their pretty start of delight and gratitude to chance, when Aunt Ellen should produce her
fairing. It would be a sad business if the poor old
lady's surprise-packet fell flat after all; and you
could not be sure, the children were capable of being
very blunt. But if their curiosity was delicately
touched and titillated, if the crisis was lightly
prepared in advance, if the occasion for a pretty
piece of manners could be a little foreseen—then
Mary counted confidently on all being well. Such
arts she had, such beautiful thought she was
capable of taking. Is a child aware of the fine
diplomacy of a loving elder, bent on securing a
creditable show from her charge? I don't believe
it escaped us—but Mary could not fail. The
children came down after tea with a look of innocence, an air of decorous affability that was indeed
for her a triumph. I forget all about it, save for a
single glimpse as clear as a miniature—a glimpse
of a very small girl with short hair, who steals
quietly into the circle of our elders, takes a seat
close to Aunt Ellen, disposes herself in readiness for
the surprise, with a mouse-like demeanour carefully
designed to show how little she suspects what is
to come. Disengaged, elaborately nonchalant, she
sits there as good as gold, waiting to be surprised
—a most artistic performance; and I hope and
believe that Aunt Ellen was gratified.

II

She was not really an aunt, she was a remoter
connexion, and no habitual figure at Earlham. I
soon forget her when I discover members of the

142

true flock, the community of Earlham, gathered in the evening light upon the lawn. Face after face appears in memory, and I should like to pause before each. And particularly of our uncles there is more to be said, for certain of them I have not yet encountered. I have seen the younger of them, the richly humoured young Olympians whom I admired and feared; but there were others, sons of our grandmother's first marriage, who in our time had their homes and households elsewhere, and who seemed to us venerable indeed. And of these not one was ever to grow old; I now know that they died in the full middle of life, in what has become their youth—it is many years ago. They lived away from Earlham, but not very far away; they often came and went, and nothing is more natural than to see one or other of them strolling across the lawn in the cool of the evening.

A small compact figure, a clean-shaven face, grey hair very smoothly brushed back from an open forehead—this is one of them, strolling with a slow and deliberate swing, his hands clasped behind his back. He came from near by, from Norwich, where he was rector of a city parish; and I wish I could make the full portrait of a very original man, gravely and humorously singular. He had a great air—a child was quickly conscious of it, as he stopped in his walk and looked down at one with composure, detached and aloof. His dignity seemed to be that of a very stately old man, and yet it was also the dignity of a humorous and ironic schoolboy, enjoying an impersonation of dry full-flavoured style. A large eye rested on one without

143

expression, there was a rather awful silence; I might begin to think him severe and formidable. Blandness was in his manner, however; there was even a touch of something suave and priestly in his appearance, in the smoothness of his grey hair, accurately parted and flattened; and then again, immediately contradicting this impression, his boyishness became the key, the clue to everything about him. Of course I interpret my vision as I did not dream of interpreting it then, long ago; but the focus of a child's eye is so precise that the image retained will always give out more and more, as one brings to it a fuller comprehension. And I now see the humour of an odd quaint boy, solemnity and irony mixed, lying close behind the slow look that was bent on us by this uncle. I have been faintly reminded of him, sometimes, when I have seen an undergraduate acting an old man's part in a play, with a mellow gravity only betrayed by the young gust and relish with which it is worn.

I cannot pretend, unfortunately, to describe what he was; he was like nobody else, and the range of his wayward unconventional mind lay far beyond the ken of a child. But at one point we could catch a hint of it, perhaps; and I find something so expressive in this single intimation that I cannot forbear to follow it for a moment. I have said already how the repute of a " ritualist " was regarded at Earlham—how the name was even capable of provoking a really sharp word from our grandfather, most benign of men. To decorate one's devotions, to clothe them in symbolic splendours, seemed to become an act that belonged to a strange inhuman world, infinitely remote from the circle of an honest home. " Incense "—and " vestments "—and " vain repetitions "—to this day I hear a certain wild unsettling strangeness in the words; I see beyond them a race of alien folk, from whom we at Earlham are safely and sharply divided. And with all this, the smoothly brushed, solemn-eyed uncle, now pacing to and fro upon the lawn with our grandfather, discussing (I think) the cricketing news—was one of them, and even excessively and luxuriantly one of them; he was indeed. There was a flight in his imagination which carried him away and away, I know not where, much beyond the conventional symbols and ornaments of the " high church "—carried him into a region where his deep originality expressed itself in forms untrammelled. He was himself alone, he could be no one else; and the fervour of his worship broke out and blossomed as it listed. And I dwell upon the memory, ghostly in the past as it may seem, because it gives me such a perfect illustration of the tone and ring of that old life at Earlham.

For a theory at Earlham, however implicitly accepted, never had the faintest chance from the moment it crossed the instinct of heavenly charity. I have seen this already, and I see it again, more clearly than ever, remembering how easily a difference, wide as the horizon, disappeared when affection willed it out of the way. Was it hard for a good " evangelical " at Earlham to understand how anybody could truly and reverently commune with the great unseen, save with a mind entirely blank and blind to the seduction of sense?—and was

it hard to believe that holy and humble men of
heart could set a value upon forms and shows that
appeared so patently vain? It was very hard,
sometimes it seemed impossible; and then the
difficulty had vanished, had utterly ceased to be,
because a heart of perfect love had suddenly passed
beyond it. I wish I could say how keen and touching is the charm of a picture that I have in mind—
deeply appealing to any one who knew our grandmother and the traditions in which she walked.
It is a picture of her at prayer and worship in her
son's church—among swinging censers and tinkling
bells and processional candles, I suppose—and she
herself serenely transcending her mere ideas and
persuasions, lifted away from the world of the
material into spaces where it no more has any
meaning, into the infinite of her love and faith.
She and her son were there together, and that was
enough.

It is an impression that is scarcely communicable,
perhaps, though I try to suggest it. But the sight
of our grandfather and this uncle on the evening
lawn, strolling and discoursing together, is more
readily seized. It is the county cricket that they
discuss, sinking enormous differences of tempera-
ment beneath their mutual respect and trust. And
still there is the quaint suspicion of something so
very youthful and fresh in the step-son, masked by
his grave composure, something that blurts out
unexpectedly at moments in his talk. He uttered
his phrase with deliberate emphasis; the forcible
word seemed to be held back by the slightest of
stammers, and then to be rapped out with decision.

IN THE GARDEN

There was a feminine group, I remember, chattering freely in the offing, with an outbreak of light shrieks and exclamations round a baby's perambulator, may be; I remember it by reason of this uncle's expression, as he was momentarily caught in the shrill tornado and detached himself resolutely, turning away to quieter companionship. " Enough of that *clack*! "—I hear the word fall with great distinctness; " enough of all that—*clack*! " It seems to me that only a schoolboy could throw quite such an old and seasoned scorn of feminine trifles into the intonation of a word.

There was an elder brother, but he was already gone; he died in the midst of a full life, and for the child at Earlham there remained only the far-away vision of a moment—a vision of a kind bearded face, dimmed with blindness (his sight had failed), a quiet presence that appeared and passed with a friendly motion. And there was a younger brother, who also was soon to vanish, but of whom my memory is plentiful—a younger brother who seemed to be always escaping, hurrying away, he too, from the buzz and clack of the company, throwing back a stammering word of apology as he fled. It was well known to me that he had a horror of small boys—which I suppose I must take to account for his attitude of flight, wherever I see him. But I didn't resent it, indeed I found it an interesting mark; very pleasing and peculiar was the manner of his hasty retreat. The company tried to tempt him back; he could perhaps be prevailed on to stay, in spite of the presence of the children, and he sat silent and flushed, with a look of uneasiness,

147

but humorously ready to meet any challenge from the rest of the party. He was short and rubicund, and he stuttered with inarticulate noises, till a remark came jerking out that had a shrewd and racy turn. And then he sat silent again, disregarding the delightful effect of his gruff retort— with just a chuckle of interior jollity when it roused somebody to a further flight. And no doubt he would soon slip away again, but he left a very clear and a very attaching and engaging imprint of himself on the mind of the child—whom I dare say he did not find so objectionable, after all.

12

The summer light of evening was perfect for Earlham. The whole radiance of the sinking sun was flung over the western lawn, blazing upon the closed blinds of the drawing-room, striking the dark ivy of the old gables, kindling the wistaria round a chimney-stack here and there to transparent green and gold. The recessed little flower-garden by the school-room windows, which had waited all day in cool retirement for its share of the sunshine, now received it straight into its lap. Golden silence, angelic peace descended upon the trees, a hush that the eternal croon of the woodpigeons in the oakwood only deepened. Whoever thinks of Earlham thinks first of the place at this hour and no other; Earlham is never so perfectly itself as it is at the full close of its wondrous day. If you cross the west lawn and look away to the river there, down the park, you see the tall trees of the heronry beginning to darken against the

light; while the willows by the water, and the oaks
and chestnuts higher up, are luminous with the
powder-gold still caught in their branches. In this
fullness of late summer the sun does not fall slanting far into the north. It sets with its face turned
straight upon the gables of the house, and the
shadows of the trees come creeping up the slope
of the park towards you, as you gaze away to the
clear gleam of the water. But there is a long hour
yet before sunset.

I could wander aside into the rough wild of long
grass that borders upon one side of this lawn. I
think I have spoken of the rain-gauge that stood
there, opening a funnel-shaped mouth to the cloud-
less sky. I liked the rain-gauge, so idle as it gaped.
in the grass through our blue days of August; and
I wondered, I wonder still, in what manner it would
mete out the change when the weather broke. The
rough ground tumbled and rose, deep in grass,
never far from the shade of scattered trees, and
as you make your way across the patch of wilderness, towards the deeper shadow, you find yourself
approaching those old sulky-seats again, and the
smooth green alley which they command. And if
it only so happened that this serene and radiant
evening had fallen a hundred years ago, as it so
easily might, there would have been a pretty
picture of life to be seen here, likely enough. It
comes into my mind through the suggestion of the
shapely tree-trunks, edged with gold, and the fine
architecture of their spreading boughs, and the
glimpses between and beneath them of the sun-
smitten gables and windows of the house. Just

149

here it might naturally chance that the artist of the family, so cunning with her pencil, would be seated over her sketch-book to seize the most pictorial of golden hours.

A century ago, then, I should certainly have come upon Aunt Richenda at this spot, plying her pencil at a great pace. She was marvellously industrious; she poured out her finished and elegant versions of the landscape with masterly fluency, never pausing or fumbling. The free lines flew over the paper, lightly sweeping the softer distance, coiling and zigzagging into the nearer foliage, digging blackly and with firm decision in the nooks of the darkest shadow. Almost while you wait the page of the sketch-book is covered; and the human interest of the scene is not forgotten either, for in the vista of the smooth alley she has placed the graceful figure of a young woman in a poke-bonnet, with a droll little skipping child by her side. And there is your sketch—" the sulky-walk at Earlham," she writes beneath it, with her initials and the date. It is the fourth or fifth, perhaps, that she has finished and signed this very day. There is not a corner, not an angle or aspect, of the house and the garden, the park and the village, that she has not recorded again and again with her sweeps and flourishes and sharp black touches—those artful twists and digs of the pencil that light up a scene and make it look like the work of the drawing-master himself. All her brothers and sisters, when they go out into the world, carry with them a collection of these delightful mementoes of the old home—an album, it may be, stamped " Earlham " on the outside, filled from

end to end by the indefatigable Richenda. They
are trophies that are valued, carefully preserved
and bequeathed to the next generation; and to
this day we may know how Richenda was occupied
on the evening of August 24, 1815. I wish we
could be quite as certain of the look of the garden
and the sulky-walk, as it lay before her in the calm
light; sometimes she strains our faith, I must
admit, with her winding paths and broken gates
and ivied walls in unlikely places; and the tree
that coils, and the tree beside it that zigzags, and
the third, just beyond, that is evenly scored with
flowing curves, are trees that I scarcely recognize
about the place as constantly as she did. But I am
grateful indeed to Aunt Richenda, and with reason;
for if doubt may be cast upon her portraits of
Earlham, the portrait of herself that is implied in
them has unmistakable truth.

She would make a very pleasing picture herself, it
is clear, as she sat over her drawing-board, critically
squaring and sizing the landscape between her two
hands, measuring it with a pencil at arm's length,
preparing to help it out handsomely with her gates
and crumbling arches if it failed to satisfy the eye
of art. What hours and hours she must have spent
in the garden on her camp-stool, with her implements disposed about her—a familiar sight to all
the friends of the household, as they strolled to and
fro with her bright-coloured, bright-haired sisters.
On a fine evening there would always be a settlement of them somewhere on the lawn, and a young
gentleman or so in attendance who had walked out
from Norwich for their society. One of these swains,

let me tell you, had arrived in his impatience at
six o'clock in the morning; it had been agreed that
he should spend a long summer's day with the
maidens of Earlham, and he might come as early
as he liked. They were ready for him, they waved
from a window and came out to him—at six in the
morning; and till nightfall they strolled and sat,
talked and read, with breakfast, dinner, supper
occurring punctually and sumptuously from time
to time. It was a great day; and the young man
had slipped into his pocket, before he started, a little
manuscript volume, his diary, and as they sat in
the shade he read extracts aloud to them, the
sparkling maidens gathering eagerly round him.
That was his chance; for to his diary, you understand, he had confided his heart, had avowed the
secret of his warm preference for one of the maidens
above the rest—and he had to read warily, to avoid
stumbling on a tell-tale passage, and more warily
still, no doubt, to make sure that the stumble, the
blush of confusion, should be noted and rightly
interpreted by one of his audience. Alas, it served
him not at all; " es ist eine alte Geschichte "—
she gave her heart elsewhere, without return, and
she died unwedded; so did the young man of the
diary—" doch bleibt es immer neu."

It all composes into an attractive scene, I think.
In stricter Quakerly circles, among the " plain "
Friends of Norwich, the sociability and the bright
complexion of life at Earlham could scarcely find
approval. The seven Miss Gurneys were much
addicted to the dance; and I believe it was Betsy
herself, great and venerable Aunt Fry, who once

in her youth appeared at meeting on Sunday in
purple boots laced with scarlet. Kitty, Betsy,
Rachel, they were the three eldest; it was at
Rachel, with her peculiar rare charm, that the
young man was careful not to glance when he broke
off in his reading, flushed and gulped and hastily
turned the page. There was a gap between the three
elder and the four younger of the sisters; but these
high-spirited children, Richenda, Hannah, Louisa,
Priscilla, easily held their own, had their share in the
dance, in the budding romances—and also in the
compunction of next day, agreeable too in its way,
when they properly searched their hearts and con-
victed themselves of vain frivolity. Kitty, the
mothering eldest, encouraged them to pause and
ponder, to turn their thoughts within; and each
of them duly kept her little journal, with its recurring burden of gay and grave. But Kitty was a
young woman of excellent sense; she on no account
permitted indulgence in the pleasures of remorse.
" Not more than four lines a day in thy journal "
was a rule she laid down at one time, finding, I
suppose, that a journal may become an excessively
sympathetic companion to a yearning penitent of
twelve. In four lines Louisa or Priscilla may dive
quite as deeply into her soul as need be.

So they all grew up under Kitty's admirable eye
to do her credit; and Richenda in particular
developed this charming talent with her pencil.
That was a gift, by all means, which should be
cultivated seriously; Richenda should have the
best of tuition. And it may easily chance that her
drawing of the sulky-walk is accomplished in the

very sight of the master; he may bend over her shoulder and criticize her foreground, her human interest, her " side-screens " and the rest of it. Mr. Crome was her master, the old original Crome of Norwich—no less. He came out to Earlham to give her lessons, he sketched with her in the park; and still in our day the house held a relic or two of his visits, apart from the imprint of his teaching that was discernible, no doubt, in Aunt Richenda's proliferation of master-pieces. The name of the distinguished old painter was always mentioned at Earlham with great respect; and everybody was pleased that Aunt Richenda's drawing-master should have been discovered by the world. She herself may surely be considered to belong to the " Norwich school." Earlham, at any rate, had warmly supported and welcomed old Crome; when the whole family-party travelled away to the north, for a holiday among the lakes and the mountains, they carried the master with them, so that the holiday was no break in the pursuit of art. Richenda, I judge, missed not a single toppling crag or mouldering ruin on their journey; she brought them all home again, duly named and signed and dated, in a trunk-load of bursting sketch-books.

13

They grew more serious, as the years of the young century increased, but not less cheerful. The purple boots were laid aside, Betsy became very " plain " indeed; all the sisters settled down to lives of exemplary purpose. But there was a fine spirit, a free humour in the family, which saved them from any blight of dull precision in their middle age; they really succeeded in gracing virtue and solid worth with a lively charm. The richest nature of them all was the young brother Samuel, soon to become a true Brother Cheeryble of the city, at whose substantial settlement to the east of London, somewhere near Stratford, I glanced a while ago. Large-hearted, large-handed, merry and shrewd and sage, he was a very worthy figure of a christian merchant. In him the genius of his family, crisply stirring and gleaming, was liberally represented. Joseph John, the brother who remained at Earlham, was of a milder habit, more subdued in pensive gravity; he was much occupied with his Quakerly "concern" (mark well the word), a call that sometimes led him far afield—to America even, more than once. Betsy found her concern in the pestiferous prison-houses which she helped to purge, Richenda (with her husband) administered and enlivened her sea-side parish. And so on with them all; and Earlham was ever in the midst of them, ready with a welcome, gathering them in again from time to time, till at last the big party diminished and there were fewer and fewer of them to meet on the great lawn.

And the mothering Kitty, meanwhile, who might well be proud of her brood—she lived always in their concerns and achievements, her brothers and sisters were her career. Rightly, I think, Joseph John should never have married, and Kitty (now ripening into " dear Aunt Catherine ") should have kept house for him at Earlham to the end. But he did marry, he even married three times; and some of his wives (not all, certainly not the last, good Eliza from America, who survived him)—the presence of some of his wives, I say, made it perhaps advisable for Aunt Catherine to have a nice little home of her own, independent of Earlham. She had one eventually; but through long years she had grown so deeply identified with Earlham that we can hardly think of her anywhere else, and in memory she is always here, the presiding genius, the gracious and dignified old lady of the Ante-room Chamber. As time went by, her motherly care extended to a growing army of young nephews and nieces; she watched them, you may suppose with what tender interest, when Earlham began to be haunted and cherished by a new generation. Brother Samuel, especially, had a large and most promising family; and he brought them often to Earlham, rumbling splendidly up to the front-door in his great barouche. They drove from London, with a night on the way at the familiar inn of Thetford; and the carriage was like a nice little home in itself for the couple of days, " lined with fawn-coloured silk," very big and comfortable with its cushions and its deep pockets and its flight of folding-steps.

Aunt Catherine was delighted to see them; Samuel's children were a beautiful party, nearly a dozen of them, I should think, in course of time. Before Aunt Catherine could turn round they were grown up, the daughters were marrying, brother Samuel was a grandfather. But the eldest son was still unmarried; and he might well be at Earlham a good deal, for he was delicate, not strong enough for the routine of his father's counting-house in London. And now I must say that Aunt Catherine had made the acquaintance of an interesting family who lived in Norwich, in the Cathedral Close—a respected clergyman, with an extremely pretty and talented wife and several young daughters; and particularly for one of the daughters Aunt Catherine had the warmest affection, gratefully returned and reciprocated by the girl herself. And that was how it came about that John Gurney, son of Samuel, married Laura Pearse and went to live at the Lodge, the old white house that abuts on the church-yard in Earlham village. John and Laura—they were living there, you remember, at the time of the death of Uncle Joseph John, when Earlham Hall stood empty after so many fruitful years. They walked round the deserted garden, looked up at the closed windows; and the young wife could not foresee that for nearly fifty years it would be she, she and none other, who to the far-scattered kindred of Earlham, young and old, would represent the spirit and the benediction of the place.

I have come round to this point again, a second time, for the pleasure of seeing how rightly and beautifully it happened that our grandmother was drawn towards the life of Earlham. They were made for each other, Earlham and she; grace and charity met together, goodness and gaiety kissed, when she came under its roof and renewed the felicity of its old story. She was a girl of seventeen when she married, and the Cathedral Close was her world; but she stepped from the household of her family with the air and mien of ripe dignity, just as

157

at Earlham, fifty years later, her laughter chimed out with the freshness of seventeen. She married, and within a very few years, as I have told, her husband died, leaving her with her young children at Earlham; she was hardly more than a girl herself, even then. Alone with her babies in that wide serenity of lawn and garden, she took up her responsibility with a natural grace that sets a spectator, at the distance of to-day, admiring and wondering anew. From somewhere, I don't know how, I receive a glimpse of her in the time of her youthful widowhood—it is in Earlham church again, on a summer morning, when the congregation stand ready to disperse at the end of the service. The big Gurney hatchment was hanging then, as it hung ever after, in the tiny transept; and our grandmother would occupy the seat within the carved oak chancel-screen where I see her so well in her age. There she would be seated, long ago, with her small brood about her; and it is so long ago, in that simple old mid-century England, that the rustic gathering of the villagers stand still in their places, yes indeed, while the young mistress of the Hall passes down the aisle, her pretty children in her hand. Serenely natural, gracefully upright and composed, she would pass down the little nave, followed by friendly eyes—any of us can clearly see that picture. Aunt Catherine, by this time at rest in her honoured grave, might well salute her as the true inheritress of the genius of Earlham.

14

That family in the Close, the daughters of the respected clergyman (not yet removed to Martham, away in the wilds)—they were indeed a rare household. There were five of them, and before they married (but they all married very soon) they were an attraction to many eyes, as they issued from the fine old gate of the cathedral precincts and crossed the open space of Tombland. Heads might be seen appearing at the windows of the bank-parlour and the solicitor's office, I have heard, when the five Miss Pearses went down the street in a posse. But on one point let there be no mistake; they were the daughters of the exquisite authoress of *Earthly Idols*, and I need not say whether or no the standard of her gentility was strict; and it follows that the society of the Close was exclusive. I don't know precisely where the rector's lady ruled her lines, but you may be sure there was no mistaking them; the bank-clerks and the scriveners might press to the window for a sight of the blooming posse, but they looked from afar. What *was* the society of the Close?—it is what I have often wondered at, thinking of our grandmother and her sisters, how from their secluded school-room they stepped into the world with their perfect bearing of composed maturity. There was the palace, the deanery, the houses of the canons—all very polite, no doubt, but you cannot say that they represented a varied range; and the education of these young ladies seemed to have been conducted under far ampler

159

skies. They had little but the example of their wondrous mother—apparently it was enough.

Great-grandmother Pearse, with her rare manner and her porcelain complexion and her romantic heart, must have looked with satisfaction upon her daughters. What would she have done if she had found herself the mother of commonplace awkward young women, destitute of charm?—she would have been deeply mortified. As it was, she might be reminded of her own blush of youth, to look at them, recognizing at the same time (as her daughters did too, perfectly) that none of them was as pretty as she. The sight of them might set her thought ranging back to the past, to the rose-leaf maiden of other days; though I suspect that she scarcely needed an impulse from without to turn her mind upon that sweet vision. It was all true—she had been, she was, a lovely creature; and I think her fancy might carry her at times, and naturally enough, far above and beyond the respected roof in Norwich Close. There was once a girl who sat by her chamber window, late at night, leaning out into the chilly darkness—looking for whom, do you suppose? Not for her lover, fleeting and false, but for death—it was for death that she waited and longed; and in her scanty white night-dress she hung out in the chill air, praying that she might catch cold and die and end her pain. The girl was she, the pretty old great-grandmother in her youth, and there was no roseate romance in her heart at that moment; but long years afterwards she might look back at the far-away vision with a stirring of emotion in which there was no more pain, in which there was even a little warmth of pride at the thought of that sweet sad picture of the past. She was the rector's lady, living in the sedate and respectable Close—she was the mother of these eager happy clear-eyed daughters; but she had known, she had known what it is to love and suffer, and under her seemly old lace and lavender silk she was still the heroine of romance. The pleasure of that knowledge remained with her undimmed, to the end of her days.

Much of her spirit survived in her daughters, I think, though in them it was changed and strengthened; they lived among clearer realities, on deeper emotions. But evidently it was to their mother that they owed the light breeze of freedom, that ripple of silver gaiety, which seems to have set through their lives and to have lasted through all the chances of their lot. It is only of one of them indeed, of our grandmother, that I can speak with a full memory; it must be chiefly of her that I think. Yet there were many echoes of them all that might easily reach us, in the air of old days at Earlham, and I well know the fresh note of originality that is ever to be recognized. There was always a difference in them, something of their own, freely irregular and conforming to no rule; I have tried to seize a glance of it here and there, in our grandmother, and I wish I could follow it further among her sisters. It would be before the image of one of them in particular, whom I have not yet encountered, that I should be tempted to linger. That one, no doubt, with her pretty graces and airs and winning ways, was the nearest in likeness to their mother; and when I recall what I can of her undying unfading charm, as fresh as ever at the end of her long life, I see a peculiar kind of distinction at its very best. A beautiful pose, a finished manner, a grace of bearing civilized and humanized in the art of life—certainly these make a distinguished impression, they may seem to represent the perfection of style. But style of that order falls short after all, as anybody can perceive when the completing touch is added to it. Perfection is reached when the finished impression is ever so lightly disturbed, deranged—when the breeze of freedom, as I call it, flutters over the worked surface, waking a movement, a shifting flaw that defeats the eye of the onlooker. That is the final flower of style, and I recognize it in my remembrance of this sister of our grandmother's. There ran through her charm a sort of tinkle and trill of natural lawlessness—it was irresistible. She easily evaded the law of time; she died full of years, but she never grew old.

15

So much it had taken, such people, such talk, such golden hours, to make our beautiful Earlham. And daily it was enriched, its tone was deepened by the deposit of new memories; no day could set without adding the full bounty of its delight to the ancient store. As the dusk thickened and the slashes of rich sunlight faded off the grass, the western gables, the topmost chimneys—even a child could be dimly aware that Earlham was more, was richer and lovelier, than it had been only

IN THE GARDEN

yesterday. There could be no dead or dull or vacant times in such a place; every turn of the hour brought its worthy contribution, and none more lavishly than the hour of sunset, when it would seem as though the senses are quicker than ever to catch the last admonitions of the day. Certainly I find it impossible, more so than at any other time, to gather and reckon the hoard of associations that live again in the twilight, round the house and across the lawn and among the darkened shrub-beries. They are everywhere at once, softly shining and calling—and I can only answer a very few.

But first there is a chatter and a crowd about the front-door, where a carriage waits for the departure of the visitors. We all collect for a friendly farewell, and there is kissing and waving, stamping and jingling, and the carriage bowls away under the blackness of the chestnut-grove. The children go scampering after it—but indeed the shadows, once you are round the corner and out of sight of the house, are lonely and solemn by now; I prefer to slip away into the open, over the short roll of the park that descends towards the church and the village. There the light comes raking across from the west, warm with the faint rose-flush of an after-glow; very still and warm and grass-scented is the air in the open, away from the trees. If you wander off in that direction you come upon the other drive, the one that marches straight from the steps of the front-door, under the towering limes, to the white gate by the church; it passes through the short tunnel of the limes, and then over the open park to the gate and the road. I find myself veering down

163

towards that gate—though really it is impossible
to suppose that I could travel so far at this hour of
the dusk; but in fancy, at any rate, I reach the
further end of the straight drive, for you get a
glimpse of the house from there which besets my
thought.

Suppose you were passing along the highway at
that point, coming from Norwich and knowing
nothing of Earlham, and you happened to pause
at the gate and glance up the straight cart-road
(I ought not to call it a drive)—here would be your
first sight of the house, so thickly the trees are
massed about it to the east; and knowing nothing
of Earlham, you divine little or nothing of what it
really is. Your eye follows the line of the cart-road,
across the open park, till it disappears in the
shadow of the lime-avenue, and between the trees
you catch this single glimpse of the house—the
front-door only, with its low pediment, and a
window or two beside and above it. It is a sight
that tells you nothing of the place; you might think
it rather formal and forbidding. The house on this
side, you remember, had been plastered over and
painted—by one of Joseph John's puritanical wives,
so we understood, who was all for keeping a house
(like herself) as plain and drab as possible. So she
had plastered the old brickwork of the house-front
and painted it a pinkish, buffish white; and the
glimpse that you had from the road gave you
nothing but the impression of an ordinary respectable mansion, a " hall " like any other, withdrawn
in gentlemanly discretion among the trees of its
park. With a considerable effort of imagination I

picture the sight as it would be seen by a stranger.
If I were the stranger I should not look twice at
the house, I should pass on down the road to the
bridge and the river.

But to us that peep of a plain bare house among
the trees had peculiar intimations of poetry. Its
aspect of solemn gentility was always connected,
you see, with the thought of arriving at Earlham.
We approached it on this side, and with that prim-
mouthed look, so untrue to itself, our Earlham
received its children. Did the house seem stiff and
ungenial in its manner of welcome? We knew
better—knew what a different expression it showed
as soon as you were fairly in its arms. There was
charm in the thought that it turned a dumb mask
to the world, revealing nothing to the casual
stranger on the highway; and the friendly freedom
and sweetness of its intimacy were enhanced by the
contrast. So to me as I stand at the gate of the
church-drive, like any chance passer-by, this appeal
of the prospect is renewed, the waft of sensation
returns—and I could revolve the thought, caress-
ingly, of all that is screened from unknowing eyes.
It is an ordinary-looking mansion, oh yes, and a few
yards down the road you come to the bridge, and
to Borrow's fishing-pool, and to a stretch of water-
meadows that are very pretty with their buttercups
and loosestrife—pass on and admire them, for you
may. But if you knew, if you knew the heart of
beauty and life and romance that lies up there
among the trees, quietly waiting, you would stay
by the gate and tenderly fondle the thought. Half
way up to the house, in the open of the park, stood

a genteel wellingtonia, and to a stranger that too,
I suppose, would wear a formal look—but if you
knew!

So it returns to me; and with this I get another
hint, expressive in its way, from the view of the
house in the distance. It suddenly looks remote
and historical—not historical in any grand sense
of the word, but with a suggestion of its placid old
durability, its power to stand on there behind its
limes, as it has stood for so long, whether we go or
come and whatever we think of it. I see how much
more history it has had than I can share, than I
can embrace with the utmost reach of my
sympathy; and I am far from resenting the touch
of aloofness which it cannot always conceal. Its
blank face *does* hide something, even from me; I
don't know who built the house, I don't know who
lived there for a hundred years and more; but the
blind background of its past may seem to make its
present familiarity the more gracious and touching
in its freedom. It had had its youth, its early
changes and chances, many of them; and all these
were forgotten and buried when the later cycle of its
romance was inaugurated. Who lived at Earlham
before the incursion of our old Gurneys in their
eighteenth-century youth? An ancient family lived
there, I just know so much as their name; but not a
whisper of a tradition ever reached us from their
time, and for us they were not. We conceived
ourselves to have appropriated Earlham so intensely that not even a ghost from its earlier past
could hold its own there. A fine pretension on our
part—and the placid face of the house might very

well send a glance of irony through the twilight, as I say the words.

No matter, I like the sense that Earlham possessed a forgotten past, buried away in the distance. I could rake up some of it even now, no doubt; and it comes back to me that the blue lady, framed in the wainscot of our grandmother's bedroom, was held to be a daughter of the earlier dynasty, so that one relic of them at any rate had survived. But it is part of the thought of Earlham, for me, that mystery and silence should obscure its origins, and I have no wish to change and re-model the thought at this late day. And when I speak of the ancient family who had inhabited the place of yore, I am reminded of the rather odd fact (I have mentioned it already) that our good Gurneys never literally and legally owned it—they never owned the house and the park, only some contiguous lands. It was a long-drawn-out tenancy, protracted over generations; and the fact was not at all without meaning for the children at our end of the chain. We were clearly aware that the house did not " belong," we believed that an alien hand might imaginably descend to clutch it away from our grandparents. I dare say there was no danger of that; but our belief assuredly gave a spice of seasoning to the mellowness of Earlham days—we felt we were leagued against the unknown. Mystery and uncertainty were thus perceptible in the air, if you cared to think of it; and you might care at times, just for the sake of the romantic effect; there was no fear of finding too much of it for comfort. If you begin to be harassed by uneasy speculations, look-

167

again—the house stands there serenely, always
ready to soothe and to re-assure. And it is certainly
strange that the chill plainness of its front should
have set me thinking of its ancient detachment;
for the plaster and white paint were comparatively
a modern mischance in its history, due to that drab-
minded great-great-aunt of our own.

16

With the shutting down of night upon the park
and the trees I part company for a time with the
child I have been following. The darkness sends
the child packing indoors; and it is a heavier spirit,
to tell the truth, that still haunts the deserted,
mist-wreathed pastures. To remember how much
had gone to the making of Earlham is to remember,
not less, how much there was to lose; a single day
in the life of the child is enough to give me the full
measure. It is all dead and gone, the place as we
knew it is buried many years deep in memory.
For us its daily enrichment, its hourly increase,
came long ago to an end; our experience of Earlham
was laid away in the past, in the form that it happened to have on a certain day, and there it has
remained. There was to be no more of Earlham for
us, from that day—no more than we already possessed. Our grandmother died, tranquilly breathing
out her beautiful life under its roof, and for us too
her death was good-bye to the place.

But good-bye?—when we can and do re-visit
the place so often and so confidently, it is not yet
time to say good-bye to Earlham. And whenever
we turn back to that memory and spend a summer's

day there again, no doubt but the hours will have added their store, will have deepened the enchantment of Earlham by nightfall; so that there is always more to possess than there seemed to be yesterday. It is so, I am well aware; and none the less among the shadows of fancy, among the wreaths of mist that creep from the river and lie in the hollows of the pasture, the mind hankers after the substance of the days dead and gone. They were no brighter, no clearer than this day of memory which I have spent among the sights and scents and voices of the garden—it is true. Yet the adventure, the uncertainty, the limitless possibility is no longer there; and I see how it is that even while I tread the grass and breathe the warm night air under the limes, there is something that I miss from of old. One's memory is *safe*—that, with all its richness, is still its incurable poverty. When I now return to Earlham and wander through my thought of the house and garden, it is always to-day and to-day only; there is no budding morrow, bringing on the unknown. This is not the Earlham that I knew, after all; the place that I knew was open to the future, one could look forward there with hope as well as backward with fond regret. Here it is that the glimpses of memory inevitably fail; they show me a closed garden, bounded on all sides, with no way open for the promise of the morrow. It is very unlike the garden that was— how unlike I well understand, when the night falls which should be bringing an unknown day. I know all the days of this Earlham of remembrance, I know them by heart.

169

EARLHAM

If I could forget the morrow in the fragrant darkness, if I could go forward under the limes in a new and strange uncertainty—that indeed would be the last triumph of a faithful memory. However dark it might be I should be sure enough of my way; I should have no need of eyes to guide me through the lime-avenue to the garden-gate, the little iron gate which leads to the dell of the weeping ash. But suppose for a moment that I could pass through the gate, hearing the well-known slam as it swings shut behind me, and wander off into the blackness of the oakwood, over the pebbly floor of its clearings and among the paper-rustle of the honesty—and all this in ignorance, in doubt of the future, such ignorance and doubt as I have not known at Earlham for so many years. It is nothing to remember all the paths and alleys and cleared spaces as exactly as I do, even though it is now pitch-dark in these recesses; I want rather to forget, to forget what the next day will bring with it, so that as I stray through the night I may be able to wonder and hope, perhaps even to fear. If that were possible, how the sense of Earlham would live again!—I should be quick to note the change from an Earlham immortal, exempt, safe out of the way of the chances of to-morrow, to the Earlham that I knew once, exposed to the future like the rest of us, living a mortal life. So only, I see, could I really re-visit the place; and this lingering and brooding over a memory that is timeless, scatheless, cannot satisfy me in the soft night-silence.

Here then is something that I have missed hitherto and that I might set myself to discover in the darkness. To forget that the story is closed, its promise fulfilled, its uncertainty at rest—to re-capture a doubt, the presence of a question unanswered—I could imagine that even this might be attainable at such an hour, in such a place. Well as I know my way through the wood, where every tree-stem meets my hand with a companionable touch, there might surely come the moment when I find myself at a loss, pausing in wonder— and at least for the moment there would be a break, no matter how trifling, in the security of the past. Yet indeed it is not conceivable that I should hesitate anywhere among these trees, and still less when I regain the open of the clear night, on the verge of the small west lawn. The glimmer of the white sulky-seats is plainly discernible, further on; the path leaves them to one side and heads forward, through more black pools and caves of shadow, to the next open space—the great lawn itself, on which so many hours of the long day have already been spent.

Well, it is not to be looked for that I should find uncertainty here, with every footstep sinking without a sound into the peace and friendliness of the grassy floor. The lawn is the very place where the past, dead and gone, seems most aloof in its immunity from time and chance. Not in musing memory, not in reflection and rumination, is it ever given us to return to the past, the real past that was a story unfinished. I cannot get there except in dreams—in dreams it is easy enough; I need the help of the dream-maker in the brain, who shuts off my knowledge of the end of the story when he begins to unroll the scene. Returning to Earlham by *that* swift flight, I recover the real true thing indeed; I may then go and come in the garden at nightfall without a suspicion of what the morning is to bring. It is the only way—fortunate that it may still be open now and then. In the mere day-dream of memory one must be content with the vividness of the image that can charm and ravish and absorb as of old, but that has no longer any power to stir with hopes and fears, disquieting and appealing. There is no help for it; memory is unassailable, a garden enclosed.

Let me then once more, before leaving the solitude of the lawn, take in the impression of its wide serenity. From the further edge of it nothing could be seen of the house, in the moonless night, but a black mass that was partly the house, partly the great tree-tops behind it; they were indistinguishably merged. House and trees together, they showed impenetrably black against the sky— a sky that was almost as dark, but of darkness open and free and distant. The spangle of stars looked faint and blurred in the mildness of the night; it was not a domed firmament that hung overhead, but the soft and yielding dimness of space. Very slowly advancing over the grass, I should gradually make out the build and form of the house, with its wings thrown forward, the deeper velvet of night between them, the pale shine of the cream-white porch in the middle. And the lights, the lights in some of the open windows—not brilliant at all in those old candle-lit days, not striking out into the darkness, but lurking shyly within, gently

and secretly glowing in a few of the rooms. Quietly
guarded, mysteriously withdrawn they seem, these
signs of life; they reveal nothing, they only hint
and lurk and suggest, holding the gaze of an onlooker. A shadow passes, a light is quenched—to
steal forth again in a moment elsewhere, in the
next room—and still it moves on, the shadow
follows, intensely silent and strange.

What lights, what windows? Suddenly into the
watchful thought of the onlooker, with a long thrill,
fell the conviction of newness, of strangeness. It
was a house unknown, never seen before—very
dimly to be guessed at, against the massing of huge
trees in which there was not a tremor of sound or
movement. Darkened rooms, and then a window-
space that glowed again, an obscure stirring of
somebody, light in hand, along the passages of the
house—it was a portent of unexplained life that
was suddenly floated into the night, isolated from
the known familiar world. There had been some
queer disconnection, the onlooker had been dropped
without warning at a particular spot, his eyes fell
searchingly upon a scene entirely new to him—so it
appeared. And yet not quite; for I am conscious
of the voice at the back of the mind which says
" Stand perfectly still, don't stir, don't shift your
eyes—or you snap the spell "; and why that check,
if the conviction of strangeness were really complete? Stand still, however, look straight, and let
the scene have its way, the miraculous dark house
where unknown lives are moving about their
business, stealthily flitting from room to room. Let
it be, let it remain so as long as it can; drink deep

of the sensation, wondering, watching, questioning the mystery. Only keep as still as the dead, and the moment will lengthen and lengthen in the alien night.

From very far away or from close at hand, I couldn't tell which, comes a breathing fragrance— or indeed it was round me all the time perhaps, it was there before I could say it had reached me. The night was full of it, a fragrance very light and pure and cool, and yet penetrating with a southern sweetness and richness. I remember well how it rests upon the windless night-air in long quiet waves; you never find it stealing round you by day, but it wakes at dusk and lingers upon the edges of the lawn, beside the flower-beds, till it vanishes again with the morning. I know it so well, I should so certainly expect it to be there, that I might easily fail to regard it for a while; but once I had caught—caught sight of it, I was going to say, for to my fancy it has a luminous satin-sheen, then it would draw me away to follow it, wherever I might be. It is the scent of a flower that opens at night-fall; and wherever I may be, that rare fragrance will always carry me straight and sure to the garden in the starshine, the garden at Earlham. Yes, the moment of strangeness, when the house and its secret glow of life within became suddenly alien and unknown, must pass with the breaking of the spell, and the spell cannot last when the night-flower opens and pours out its silvery sweetness. All the memory of Earlham comes welling back into my thought again; the strange house in the night is so little strange that I seem from all time to have

174

known every corner of it. Earlham it is, with a light
glowing here and there behind the familiar windows
—there the nursery, that one our grandmother's
room, here the Ante-room Chamber among the
dark leafage of climbing vines and roses. Could I
ever have the sense of a mystery, an unknown
secret lurking there among the moving shadows?
I know them by heart, I have known them from all
time.

Ah but none the less I have found what I was
looking for; it *can* be found after all, and not only
in dreams. It was just a flash of sensation, not
more, but I recognized it at once. Wait however—
wait and look nearer at the flower-beds, which lie
in a rambling cluster, you remember, under the
lip of the steep bank of grass. Their coiling ser-
pentine forms are all confused in the darkness,
but I can easily thread the narrow grassy paths
that separate each from each. The bright colours
of the geraniums and the salvias are veiled by night;
the brightest red and blue, even the flaring orange
of the marigolds, are softened and obscured so that
you hardly notice them among the deep grey of the
tufts and bushes. But wait—the scent of the night-
flower leads me on, where the narrow way between
the beds goes turning and twisting. And there—
where this morning you saw nothing but tall stalks,
broad leaves, drooping and discoloured flower-
trumpets, look now! Pure and cool and snow-white
the clear stars have opened with the fall of the dusk,
and whiter and whiter they grow as the night
deepens. This is the flower which sends that wave
of fragrance into the stillness, the flower that shines

175

in the garden at Earlham from dusk to dawn. Far into an August night, till the first quiver of day-break stirs the hush of the darkness, the white stars hang motionless on their tall stalks, facing to the sky. With the daylight they droop and fall; but in August the morning already delays, there are long hours after midnight before the polar clouds begin to catch the advancing light. Till then the night-flower blooms in its white splendour, awake and alone.

And I found what I was looking for, most strangely, in the moment of recall to Earlham by the scent of the flower. " I have never been here before," I had said to myself out there on the lawn —as one does, for no reason at all, on the spot where one has stood a thousand times. " What shadows are those behind the windows? " And then, as the presence of Earlham returned with that fragrance, I had *forgotten*—quite forgotten that the place was dead and gone, that I shall never see it again, that no day ever breaks there with new promise, new hopes and fears. The small sweet shock of finding the house so familiar again was enough; it banished everything from my thought but the fresh and sharp delight of recognition. Just for the flash of a moment I felt that it was the old Earlham, as it used to be, with still undiscovered experience before it—not this safe, secluded, im-mortalized Earlham that I possess in memory. And it was all the stuff of a day-dream—strange that it should so be possible to pile life upon life, each with its distinct and clear-cut illusion. The day-dream of memory took me to the lawn, in a

night of summer long years ago; and once there,
I could be visited by the illusion of strangeness—
just as it might have befallen me of old, on such a
night; and into that illusion there broke the
immediate sense of a living Earlham, where anything yet may happen—Earlham as it really was.
It shows how memory is to be trusted; memory
will give one everything, will even give one, at the
right hour, the chance to forget the unnatural
security in which it guards the past. An August
night, the scent of a flower—I remember these, and
for a moment they enable me to look forward to a
morrow, big with uncertainty as of old, that begins
to dawn upon the garden at Earlham, already
whitening the highest of the high-towering clouds.

III: OUTSIDE AND BEYOND

I

THE river at Earlham was simply the river; I never thought of its possessing a name upon the county-map. It does possess one, however, and a name not undistinguished among the waters of East Anglia—the river Yare. Early in its course it reaches Earlham; it twinkles over gravel and water-cress to the brick archway of the bridge, turns suddenly black and silent in the fishing-pool, and winds idly away through the Earlham meadows, a full-fed stream, deep enough to carry us in our broad-beamed old boat. Upstream we could not penetrate far; we should soon hear the floor of the river grinding upon our keel. But downstream the waterway is open to us as far as Cringleford mill— quite as much of a voyage as we shall wish to cover and re-trace on a fine hot morning.

So at last we may dip down to the sunk fence beyond the west lawn and journey away towards the water-meadows. The park, gently falling to the valley, had the dignity of its fine trees, scattered and grouped here and there; but when you are fairly out on the slope you can hardly call it a real park; it is quite small, it quickly lapses into flat green meadow-land—and here is the pond. Rustling with rushes, starred with water-lilies in the open, the pond would be sure to delay me; it had many attractions, the best of them perhaps the ancient willow-trunk, rooted in the soft bank,

179

which had sunk and sunk as it leaned over the water, till at last it lay at full length upon the surface, with the lily-leaves floating against its bark. A large and beautiful pond it certainly was; it spread out quite near the river, but there was a stretch of thick grass between the two; and so we should skirt round the pond, to reach the boat-house by the thorn on the river-bank. But you cannot neglect the willow-trunk on the way; there seemed always a chance that if you scrambled and sprawled to the end of it you might find that a white water-lily had unfolded within reach of a grabbing hand. It never had; it was so near that you could see the little black-beetles among its golden spikes, but there was no getting possession of it. What should I do with a water-lily, if I did succeed in clutching the stalk? I couldn't say; yet it would be a valuable prize, the thought of it snapping juicily between my fingers is somehow alluring. And then there are the steel-blue dragon-flies, darting and glancing, and there is the yellow fleabane— and then there is the deep shade of the wood that marches to the very verge of the pond, at the further end of it. Remember this wood of great trees; I say no more of it for the moment, for the boat-house on the river is close at hand, and we all crowd thither and cluster about the low doorway.

Within there was thudding and bumping and lurching, splashes of echoing water, shafts of green twilight; the boat swayed and smacked its lips (so you might say) as we bundled in and disposed ourselves. Somebody stood in the bows to unlock the gate; and it burst open, caught by the stream outside, and the boat pushed forth into the blaze of light, the water-cool breezes, the clean smell of the draggled weeds. Light and air, the silent movement, the wild and nameless fragrances—they make a penetrating experience. The water talked beneath us as the boat swung round into the stream; and immediately the familiar landscape was changed before our eyes, the fields and woods beyond the low banks seemed to have drawn apart with a new character. Committed to the flow of the stream, one looks back on the green world as though one had left it; to float upon water is as detaching, as liberating as to soar in air. Those woods, that flat marshland, now belong to another sphere; I survey it with curiosity, almost wishing to return to it already, so inviting it seems to enterprise and discovery. But here meanwhile is the sphere of the water-world, with its strange and lovely treasures; trailing my hands in its delicious chill, I can soon be lost in the landscape of the river-floor.

Shallow and pool, pool and shallow, the river coiled its way through the hollow land. Outside the boat-house the gravelly bottom was full in view, only blurred a little by the twist and swirl in the clear glass of the water. Do you know that broad-leaved plant, bright green, translucent, that grows in thick drifts along the bed of the stream, never touching the surface?—and the fine feathery thing, a darker green, eternally pulled by the current, like a thicket through which a wind never ceases to blow?—and the stalks of the arrowhead, that climb to the upper air and are shaken there by a constant little breeze, it would seem, which is not really a breeze but the same secret tug of the stream below?—and the perpetual flitting of tiny shadows over the gravel and sand, as the minnows dart from under our monstrous hull, the leviathan that pushes among their cressy islets? The only sound in the quiet valley was the measured cluck of our clumsy old rowlocks; the reedy pastures were deserted, there wasn't a house or a cottage in sight; the tawny cows stood stock-still, solemnly eyeing us as we passed. And then, as we steered round a swinging bend of the river, the sunlit floor had disappeared and there was nothing but blackness beneath us, thick darkness of water unbroken by reed or rush—a deep pool, and you could plunge the oar down and down, further and further into the bottomless mud; and the next moment, perhaps, the boat was almost scraping the clean gravel again, and the smooth bottle-green reed-stems stood out into the water away from the bank; and so the river went winding on its leisurely way, and after ever so long you still saw the boat-house within easy hail, just across the breadth of a single meadow.

There was a reed-bed that appeared very soon on the right, a patch of swamp covered densely with those great reeds like gigantic blades of grass, each with its mop of pinkish plume streaming in the wind. A small jungle of undrained swamp, tangled with thorn-bushes—I take a deep interest in it by reason of an unforgettable passage in the past. Mark the great flattened platform of dead rushes, close to the water's edge, almost hidden by the plumy reed-forest. It is the nest of a swan—empty now and abandoned, to be sure; but if you had come here earlier in the year you would have been met in mid-stream by the master of the place, the hissing and ruffling swan, and you might well have thought twice before you faced his challenge. I, let me tell you, had faced it; but I admit that I had had powerful support. We were not often at Earlham in birds'-nesting time; and the thrill was the keener when I did get the chance, twice or thrice, of an adventure among the birds of the swamp and the water-meadow. For the quest of the swan I had the company of friend Sidell the butler—the man of nerve, of cool and masterful decision. He met and confronted the passionate fowl with a composure that disconcerted it entirely, and I followed him in easy confidence.

The swan breathed fury, puffing out his magnificent wings; and then he was quite taken aback by Sidell's assurance, and could only sail helplessly to and fro, pouting and hissing, while we landed at the nest; and somehow we must have dislodged his mate, for I remember the sight of the great discoloured eggs, three or four, that lay in the high-piled nest. If it should appear that one of the eggs was addled I had leave to take it; but how are you to know whether an egg is addled while the bird is still sitting hopefully on them all? It is possible, I held, to make certain by shaking the eggs sharply, one by one; the good egg gives no sound, the ripening chick is firmly embedded within; but in the bad you can hear the slop and jumble of the rotting contents, from which no offspring is to be expected. I applied the test accordingly, and one of the eggs was at any rate addled by the time I had done with it. I bore it off, and I have not forgotten the afternoon that was spent in draining the huge malodorous shell. So to you I have discovered (you recognize the quotation) that swan's nest among the reeds.

2

Mrs. Browning's poem is nearly all about knights and pages and prancing horses; I doubt if she had ever really seen the nest of a swan. But I can tell of yet rarer things, once I am with Sidell among the birds. We made a marvellous excursion one April day to a certain mere, a lake full of swampy islets, to which the black-headed gulls return every year in their thousands, never learning better than to lay their eggs at the very feet of the depredator. You approach the lake by winding bowery lanes; it is quite in the manner of Norfolk to mask its waters about with great trees, with long turnip-slopes, so that you may follow the shady lane from village to village without detecting the hollow of secluded marshland that you skirt and pass by. The mere of the gulls, I seem to remember, thus lurks in the midst of an ambling tree-scattered country-side; and we stopped at a gate in the lane and turned aside by a woodland path like any other, which gave no hint of what we should see in a moment. So it comes back to me; and presently a sheet of water opened before us, at the edge of the wood, and there was the hidden haunt of the swarming, screaming birds.

Their eggs are taken, and they lay more; and

these are taken, and they lay more again; and I forget how often the robbery is repeated, but it stops just in time to avoid discouraging them altogether. They think it a fatality that must be borne; with the third or fourth nest-full of eggs they cheat their destiny, they rear a family, but the earlier attempts are foredoomed. Year after year they brave the curse that lies upon the mere; they scream and splutter over the punctual strokes of fate; and yet they persevere, and they take credit, I dare say, for their cleverness in evading the fourth or fifth. The keeper of the mere and his minions pack the eggs into boxes and despatch them to those who know what is good to eat in April. When we reached the lake-side the gulls were crying out for the ten-millionth time that such things ought not to be allowed. We found a boat, and we rowed across the open water to an island trodden and littered by many generations of the long-suffering birds; they were all about us, with their bright eyes and their flashing wings and their decent little brown spring-hoods. The day's robbery had been achieved; but here and there a spotted egg, green and brown and black, might be found on the bare spongy floor; and perhaps it was the first time I had ever known the joy of a bird-haunted marsh in breeding-time. With the birds that flutter and chirp, that hop on lawns and whisk among the bushes and patter through the dead leaves—with these I was familiar, but not with the birds that flap and scream, that paddle jerkily into the cover of the reeds and stamp the mud-bank with their neat triangular footprints. So this was always a famous day, the first day among the gulls and the dabchicks and the coots of the mere.

And as soon as I speak of it I am caught by the memory of another and later day, and another blue-green forest of rustling reeds; and I remember how, in a very small flat-bottomed boat, one might cautiously push along the narrow water-way that twisted and turned, deep among the great feathery stalks—cautiously, silently, with ear and eye strained and alert. These other solitudes, more remote than the mere of the gulls, were haunted by certain charming and distinguished little creatures, for whom I was ready to wait and watch by the hour. It was late in the summer, and there was very little stirring of life around the boat—scarcely more than the shuffle and flap, here and there, of a startled moor-hen; nesting-time was over, the population of the reeds had fallen shy and silent. But not entirely silent, it seemed—for I heard a note, near and far, that was like the striking of a very small silver gong, a note I had never heard before. It was enough to set one's eye travelling keenly among the forest of the stalks; the clear note was uttered on this side, near at hand, and then it seemed to be far ahead of me, close behind me; and again and again I had surely been just too slow, had barely missed the flit of a wing across the open water-way. And then at last, quietly rounding a corner, I saw them full, a pair of them— they gleamed and passed and disappeared among the rushes. Shining, straw-golden little birds they were, carrying long wedge-shaped tails behind them; they were bearded-tits, and through the hours of the

afternoon I saw not a few of them, and the tiny
clang of their call-note was constantly about me.
The flight of time is forgotten when I have seen
and heard the bearded-tit; I can attend to nothing
else, I follow the gleaming bird further and further
into the midst of the mere.

3

But I am concerned with the river at Earlham,
where it wound through the water-meadows; and
after passing the thicket of the swan's nest one
should begin to notice carefully the long wood of
great trees that accompanies our journey. It strides
down the valley, on the left hand, a hundred yards
or so from the river; it is still the wood I spoke of
just now, the wood that shadowed one end of the
lilied pond. It is the heronry; and in those branching tree-tops you may see the dark piles of the nests
to which the herons return in the spring. It was a
dwindling colony, I fear; we could not count more
than a dozen nests, perhaps; and in August of
course they were all deserted—we rarely had the
luck of surprising a heron by the water-side and of
watching its lordly voyage down the sky. But it
was truly a heronry, that wood—I hope it is still;
and we knew no other, and we felt it to rank among
the proudest of the glories of Earlham.

The wood marched on down the valley, never far
from the river; it was a dense and tangled forest,
long and narrow, and it was crossed in the middle
by a cart-track that went tunnelling through the
leafage. The cart-track divided the kingdom of the
herons from that of the rooks; they scrupulously

respected each other's domain. Very soon, as our
boat pushed forward, the rooks were wheeling and
braying their loudest overhead. The sky was full
of flapping wings, those foolish up-curved, open-
quilled wings that seem so badly designed for riding
the air. The voices of the rooks awoke the valley—
for all this time there has been no sight of a human
being, there never was, in these solitary pastures;
it was only our lumbering boat, so it seemed, that
ever disturbed their peace. We drifted down and
down between the low banks; and presently the
wood of the rooks ended abruptly, and to right and
left we could see the expanse of the shallow valley,
between the mild slopes and swellings that in
Norfolk are counted as hills. From our low level,
looking across the water-meadows, we could discover no break in the green flats of the pasture;
only here and there an isolated wooden gate, with
nothing on either side of it, stood up oddly in the
midst of the grass—betraying, you see, the lie of
the hidden dykes that separated field from field.
The gate marks the spot where the dyke is crossed
by a culvert or a bridge of wooden planking; and
I dare say the thought of the dykes, big and little,
full of reeds and frogs and various treasure, may
bring our boat to a standstill, and we may dis-
embark for an oozy, juicy scramble among the
fleabane and bog-beans and forget-me-not.

But our voyage was far from its end. On and on
we went, past the pollard-willows, past the two
skeleton windmills that pumped the river-water, I
suppose, up the swelling hill towards Eaton—and
soon the stream became rapidly deeper, and houses

appeared, clustered about with trees, and a bright trim garden or two descended to the river-bank. Cringleford (pleasing name) was in sight; we floated upon a deep pool that even in the blaze of noon you might feel to be treacherous and sinister. For look ahead, see the picturesque building that straggles across the river and blocks the way, note where the river disappears beneath it. That is Cringleford mill; it opens a dark jaw and swallows up the stream—quite quietly, without a sign of warning; and we are well aware that it is a place of extreme peril. I think we must have read or heard of a " mill-race," how it snatches the unwary, draws them in and destroys them in the darkness, where the great wheel hungrily pounds and grunts. And though the pool of Cringleford seemed so peaceful, so innocently dreamful in the sun, we had no doubt that danger lurked; we floated watchfully, with a cautious eye for that wide and evil slit of a mouth in the distance, opening with a black grin upon the verge of the water. Nearer we ventured, a little nearer—but then it was time to remember our return-voyage, the long pull upstream that still awaited us.

The Yare seems a leisurely current till you begin to breast it in a heavy old boat under a high sun. It starts into activity then, I can assure you; the oar that you have gaily plied in the descent becomes hostile and hateful, the boat a leaden tub; now is the time for your elders to exert themselves, while you recline with dignity in the stern and handle the rudder-strings. I like to be free to watch the shifting landscape, I like the responsibility of steering

189

our course; there is something noble and serene in
the attitude of the helmsman, surveying the effort
of the crew, which appeals to me more keenly than
I should care to admit. I cannot be surprised if my
manner betrays a natural authority, as I lean
negligently back in my place, drinking in the
familiar scene, and pull the alternate strings that
send us sweeping round the bends of the river.
A royal passage upstream, while the slaves bend
to the oars—and quicker than you could believe
possible the nose of the boat darts at the bank,
rams itself firmly into a slush of mud, and the
helmsman is exposed to the free-spoken jeers of the
crew.

The shady bank, however, of the reach just below
the little windmills has associations that make me
forget my discomfiture. Here were fine old willow-
trunks, branching thickly, and they bring a picture
of memory to the light. It was just the place for a
picnic—it had been tried and proved more than
once. Not at this time of day, not at high noon,
but towards tea-time we had more than once
landed by the willows with hamper and kettle;
those were days that stood out in remembrance for
many reasons. And one of the reasons seems to
have been that exactly on those afternoons, those
only, the golden weather was chilled and clouded;
the sun always blazed at Earlham, surely, save
when we landed with uncles and cousins on the
river-bank, far from home, and prepared to collect
sticks, build a fire and boil our kettle. Then the
clouds gathered, rain threatened, wind whistled—
the scene is vividly before me. People looked

doubtfully at the sky and the grass, spread mackin-
toshes, huddled and shivered; but the children
were not discouraged, for that was the way of an
Earlham picnic, one would not wish to improve
upon it. The centre of the scene is one of our
uncles, crouching on hands and knees over a fire
that he tends and coaxes, screening it from the gust
with a wall of tilted umbrellas round which he peers
with whimsical looks; the children hover about and
gaze at him with sudden chuckles.

Rain and wind mattered nothing to us—we had
our picnic. The joy of it was twofold. In the first
place it was traditional; regularly, on our return
to Earlham, the question of a water-picnic appeared
among our schemes, fitting into its turn like a piece
of ritual; so it always was, so it ever should be—
these children were resolute precisians in such a
matter. And then there was another savour in a
picnic; and I am almost shy of returning yet again
to the romance of an eight-year-old appetite, but
how can I forget the brilliance of the eating in those
conditions? A bun or a sandwich on its plate at
nursery-tea is admirable; but wrap it up in white
paper, make a neat parcel of it, carry it off with you
for a long afternoon, and finally consume it in a
boat or on a river-bank—poetry has passed into it
by that time, and to a child it is a fact that poetry
tastes. Transubstantiation, to a child, is no mere
venture of faith; it is a matter established by the
senses, like any other; and though I cannot verify
it now, I perfectly recall the new flavour of the
sandwich that has been spiced and seasoned by
new surroundings. And even more potent in its

influence than a boat and a river is a railway-train,
a crowded compartment in which a hamper is
unpacked and small parcels in butter-stained white
paper are handed round—lunch in the train, one of
the richest of all the incidents in the long ecstasy of
the journey to Earlham. You know how it happens;
one climbs into the corner by the window to watch
the racing trees and telegraph-poles, and the hours
loiter, and the elders of the party sit mutely nursing
their headaches (you remember their train headaches), and there is a fragrance of eau-de-cologne, of
morocco travelling-bags, of begrimed upholstery;
and at last, at last it is time to open the hamper, to
unpack the sandwiches; and for my part I feel I
could munch my way through them for an hour, and
then be ready to begin all over again. I have fed
on poetry; and I am glad to think I made such use
of the opportunity that the flavour is distinct to me
after many years.

As for the voyage upstream in the beating sunshine, the later stages are blurred with a luxury of
somnolence; it is clear that I have relinquished the
rudder; I keep no count of the twists of the river,
I lose myself in the rhythmical cluck and splash of
the oars. On and on, cluck and splash—and at
length we are wheeling and lurching into the cool
shadow of the boat-house again; and now comes the
endless toil of the walk up the park, an almost
impossible anti-climax to our adventure. Up there
among the trees are the gables and chimneys of
home; but the slope of the park seems to refuse to
grow less, as one trudges and stumbles among the
scorched tussocks of the grass. But suppose that

one clings to an ever-companionable arm, demanding one of those strange and beautiful stories of which I have spoken already—why not indeed, for the thirtieth time, the story of the tapioca-pudding and its burial in the shrubbery? It is well; time and space are obliterated while the drama gathers and breaks; we find ourselves in the shade of the west lawn just as the bell peals out to call us indoors —five minutes before luncheon-time.

4

Except to the river we should not very often travel beyond the garden—partly because the garden was eventful enough for a life-time, partly because adventure could not be improvised, extemporized, in the outer world. To penetrate there was a matter of plans and public arrangements; our elders must co-operate, and they may be willing and sympathetic, but their interest in a project puts it at once among formal, discussible things, whereas the peculiar charm of a private enterprise is that it needs no explanation. None the less we should welcome the prospect of an afternoon in Norwich with our grandmother; when she drives " in," carrying us with her, we are very ready to bring the fine old city into our game, so to speak, to include it in the life and legend of Earlham.

As I think of Norwich I remember first how the carriage-horses seemed to fill the narrow channel of London Street, how their hooves pounded and echoed on the wooden pavement, how Patrick the coachman, from his height, steered them with easy supremacy through the jostle of smaller traffic.

EARLHAM

The shops of London Street were very brilliant, and we stopped here and there, and Patrick beckoned with a flourish of his whip to the salesman within, who issued with friendly smiles to confer with our grandmother, taking his place at once thereby, to my sense, in the family party of Earlham. There were friends everywhere to greet us, and the horses twisted their way without hesitation round the sharp turns, swept up and down the scooping slopes and pitches of the old streets. The heart of Norwich, in the region about the market-place, has a very distinguished air. It impressed me with the dignity and the grand style of a capital city, much more of a city and a capital than London itself, which was merely a chance aggregation of streets. Norwich had a personal, self-conscious look, aware of its own being; it was from Norwich, not from London, that one could learn to think of a city as a body of life and character. By the time our carriage had threaded a dozen narrow ways and worked up the hill to St. Stephen's, to St. Peter's, I was filled with pride in the familiar and kindly bond that united us to such a memorable friend.

St. Peter's Mancroft—it is a good civic church, standing very stately above the market-place; one might catch sight of its dominating tower and spire at many points of our course. And its odd old name made one begin to peer and watch for the perpetual church-towers of the Norwich street-corners and to demand their names too—in half an hour one may collect a curious store. Our grandmother knew them all; no tower or street of Norwich, I suppose, was without its quick associa-

tions for her. She named the churches, and already
in very early days I had them by heart: St. Michael-
at-Plea, St. Michael-at-Thorn, St. Martin-at-Oak,
St. Miles Coslany, a lengthening catalogue of picturesque titles that stirred the imagination with
many thrills. Churches, timbered houses, the
ancient guildhall of black flint, they all crowded
upon us with romance; sitting on the small back-
seat of the carriage, facing our grandmother, I
should crane half-bewildered from side to side,
fearful of missing a single glimpse of these wonders.
If I try to discern exactly what they can have
meant to an excited child, with no knowledge
whatever of their historic life, I certainly see nothing
but a blank. Our dear grandmother, familiarly
as she moved through the city, had no improving
information to offer us; she was quite as innocent
of facts and dates as I was myself. But that was
fortunate; all we needed was the beautiful names,
anything more would have oppressed our fancy;
and really I think I principally enjoyed, not the
presence of the past, but the grand sense that in the
midst of this antiquity we were quite at home and
at our ease—the sense that the city with all its pride
was for us but an appanage of Earlham. When I
remembered this, I did my best to look benevolent,
superior, careless; it was all a very old story to *me*,
I implied, but it was pleasant to cast a glance upon
it in passing, to throw a wave of the hand to the
well-known scene. And I was conscious indeed of
the difficulty of reconciling this attitude with the
ingenuous eagerness that set me bouncing to and
fro on the back-seat, as we rattled through the open

spaces of the cattle-market and beheld the immense
Norman keep of the Castle on its mound.

But it was when we descended to the lower parts
of the city, towards Tombland and the cathedral,
that the charm of intimacy was at its best. Oddly
enough—or naturally enough, I dare say—I could
not take the faintest interest in the cathedral for its
own sake; I remember standing at the west door,
gaping up at the bossed tracery of the vault, with a
mind emptied of all activity, struck limp and lifeless
by a spectacle too big for it. I could do nothing
with the cathedral as an object of beauty and
interest; it soared above me, swooped and bore me
down. But when I turned away and strolled with
grandmother through the Close, and she pointed
out the home of her childhood, spoke of the bishop's
palace and the deanery, led me to the old ferry and
the grey bits of ruinous wall and archway by the
river—when the towering cathedral, there behind
us, became part of her story, part of daily life and
familiar habit—then indeed I took possession of it
with perfect assurance. I could include it, I could
embrace and patronize the good old cathedral,
when it was thus pulled into the pattern—the
pattern of Earlham, as I keep on discovering it.
I stepped out beside the daughter of the Close, to
whom the overwhelming great church was a fact
as simple and homely as Sunday morning, quite
prepared to master all the vastness of antiquity in
that fashion. And I now see that just in that way
and no other a child could handle and use the
impression of ancient beauty; our grandmother
glanced at it affectionately, as though at a faithful

companion, and I at her side was delighted to do the same. We neither of us distracted ourselves by trying to understand it.

"This is Pull Ferry," she said, when we reached the river-bank at the lower end of the Close. There it was, I suppose, that the barges were towed and moored, laden with the stone that built the cathedral and the monastery; there was the quay where the monks of the priory received and landed their supplies. Of all that I had no notion at all, not even enough to make me wonder and ask questions about the grey old gateway and broken tower. We stood and looked for a minute, and then we turned back into the Close, and grandmother had a message to leave or an enquiry to make at the house of a canon; and as if it had happened this morning I remember how the charm of the place suddenly flowered out all round me while I waited, moving me to unspeakable tenderness. What I liked about it was not in the least its beauty, but simply the fact that it was mine, and had been mine for so long. I had never seen it five minutes before; but grandmother's tone, when she spoke of it, was full of a lifelong intimacy that I could share on the spot.

5

There was plenty of business to transact in Norwich before we were ready to return home. It was necessary first to drive round by the fish-market; there we seemed always to be expected, and as soon as the carriage paused an aproned young man darted forth with a bundle or basket, discreetly packed, and bestowed it under the coach-

man's box. That was the fish for dinner; and
Patrick, it was probable, had many other commis-
sions entrusted to him by Mrs. Chapman, and
gradually the carriage was stored with various goods.
Moreover we had started from Earlham, I need not
say, with the usual assortment of packages and jars
and baskets under all the seats, and for anything
that we took in there was something no less substantial to give out. Our course took us hither and
thither among the outlying streets of the city; we
learned to know a good many of the doors at which
we habitually stopped. Our grandmother's circle
of friends was very large, and there was an
attractive parcel, likely enough, for all the poor
things and the good souls in turn.

I pause in remembrance before a door that we
seem to have frequented regularly for many years.
It was in a prim street of tiny houses, not unsightly;
and here we all got out of the carriage and went in
to call upon Mrs. Cook. We climbed to her bed-
room—for there she lay helpless, year by year,
always greeting us with the same dreadful, high-
pillowed, gaunt fascination. She lay there like a
wild old witch, beaten and brought low, but surely
still capable in her imprisonment of a stealthy spell
or so if she had the mind. That was how this
amiable, humble, grateful old person (as I suppose
she was) struck a child; it was impossible to believe
that her cries and chirrups of delight at our appearance had no sinister meaning. So we stood by her
bed and stared at her, appalled and attracted,
while grandmother explained us to her, named and
placed us in a family whose ramification she followed

with faithful interest. She didn't remember us very well from visit to visit; and I never forgot that one of our uncles (the wickedest) had once taken a perfect stranger to see her and had introduced him to her as one of ourselves—to her intense satisfaction, for she declared she would have known the gentleman anywhere for his likeness to the rest of us. Was that a cruel fraud to practise on the poor soul, or a kindness to offer her?—I had heard the question debated, and I remembered our grandmother's " Don't, dear—don't! "—unwilling to be amused, while she smiled at a story that lost nothing in our uncle's telling. It added another note of curiosity to the sight of Mrs. Cook.

But what I chiefly notice, as I recall how grandmother greeted and talked to her, is something not at all easily to be described. It is the attitude of the charming and tender and bountiful visitor towards the sad old wreck who lay there on the pillow and mumbled her gratitude and folded her skinny fingers round the kind hand. A child, of course, had no notion how our grandmother's genius was revealed at such a moment; but from this distance of time I see it fill the room with a wonderful radiation. And I can't, when I try to speak of it, tell where to begin; for the whole of her nature was warmth and quickness and light, and there were no qualities, no virtues in it that were not all-pervasive, liberated, transmuted into spirit and flame. When they are withdrawn and defined they seem no longer like her—no more than a handful of salt is like the blue suffusion of the fire into which it is thrown. To describe a character like this, naming

its qualities one by one, gives it far too much of an
air of deliberation, of formal structure, as though
it were composed and compacted of different
materials laid together. Her manner of being was
as little of that kind as could be; it escapes the
words that would close upon it.

Let me say at least that she possessed, mingled
with the utter simplicity of her charity, a pretty
strain of stateliness, of worldliness—which kept Mrs.
Cook in her place, not a doubt of it, even while they
spoke together and smiled and prayed in the light
of a love where none was afore or after other. Our
grandmother, tending her suffering friends, moved
among them entirely as one who serves—absolutely
forgetful of herself, lost in the instant free flow of
her sympathy; she forgot, for she had no need to
remember, the distinctions that here and now, in the
world as it is made (and providentially, unquestion-
ably made), have the meaning and the force that we
recognize, whatever we think of them. She had
no need to remember these things because she did
not question them; it is we, the rest of us, asking
why Mrs. Cook should lie bed-ridden in a dull street
and a frowzy little room—it is we who cannot meet
her as an equal and a sister, cannot serve her
simply, cannot feel at home among her dingy relics
and imitations of gentility. Who are we, and what
is Mrs. Cook?—we don't know, and we know we
don't know, and the unanswered questions visibly
plague us; Mrs. Cook herself is only too well aware
of the fidget of their presence, and the end of it is
that we go away without having been with her,
really and comfortably with her, for a moment of

our visit. But look at Mrs. Cook when our grandmother enters the little room with radiance, with
gaiety in her voice, with that sweet trembling harp-
note of tenderness in her greeting—it is a christian
soul that meets another, without the semblance of a
barrier between them; no doubts or delicacies or
compunctions divide them, they join hands in
perfect understanding. And yet it is as clear and
natural as day to both of them that in the world
they are far apart; and here, where they meet, one
of them brings sympathy and bounty, the other
gives gratitude, and the disparity of the exchange
never troubles them in the least. It is part of the
order of things, and they can disregard it as easily
as we allow for the daily cataclysm of sunset and
nightfall. Suppose that every evening, with the
closing-in of the dark, we should blame the monstrosity of allowing the sun to sink; that would
seem to Mrs. Cook quite as reasonable as to ask why
in the world she should lie there in her old flannel
bed-gown, staring at the cheap wall-paper a few
feet away from her, while we drive home through
the radiant afternoon to Earlham.

And our grandmother—she could suffer in all her
vibrating heart with the sufferings of the poor and
the forlorn, the woes of the world in distress were
her own; but it was no part of her thought that in
comforting and succouring the poor, who are always
with us, we should begin to be sceptical or ironical
about the distinction between Earlham and the
humble abode of Mrs. Cook. She believed in the
distinction, took it as real and lasting; no words
were needed, but without words she made it un-

mistakable that everybody had his due station and degree. In that degree he might be miserable and destitute, and then the more fortunate had the duty and the joy of hastening to his rescue; still his degree remained, and theirs too, and nothing in the sincerity of Christian fellowship would lead to obliterating the difference. See her, for example, when half-way home, on the high-road, she suddenly calls to the coachman and stops the carriage—a tired woman with a baby is trailing on foot in the dust, and we can give her a lift on the way. " Jump in," cries grandmother, smiling and beckoning; and she makes room beside her, and the woman's slight surprise and confusion quickly disappear in easy talk about her journey, her home, her ailing child. I can clearly see her anxious, strained face as she responds, more and more readily; and before we reach home and it is time for her to set off on her tramp again, grandmother will doubtless have contrived some means of solidly and sympathetic-ally helping her, and the woman goes on with the knowledge that she has made a friend. And in the whole transaction our grandmother has the fine style, the serene gesture of a princess, even while she enters the life of the poor pilgrim with the eager simplicity and participation of a saint. At least it is something like that—if only these definite words and phrases seemed at all to suggest the living light of her spirit.

6

We drove out of Norwich then, on our way home, as the afternoon grew golden towards tea-time.

OUTSIDE AND BEYOND

Before leaving the city we should not forget to look with interest, in passing, at the big tower of St. Giles's church; for it was at St. Giles's, you remember, that our grandfather had formerly ministered for so long. It was a church, therefore, that peculiarly belonged to Earlham, though the days of the intimate association between the two were pretty well beyond our memory. The legend of those years still survived for us, however, and I know exactly how at Earlham, on Sunday morning, the household would dispose itself for the journey to church. Who wants to drive in?—who will walk? —the question ran round the breakfast table and the parties were made up. In those days you naturally wore your best on Sunday; but your best, though it was brighter and crisper and tenser than week-day wear, would be " suitable," with no fly-away feathers or fancies, and I see how the ladies of the party, when they assemble in the hall, touch and pat the bows of their bonnet-strings and ease the set of their veils. They would gather in the hall with their prayer-books and their parasols, and some of them would set off on foot with our grandfather and our uncles, and presently the carriage would come round for the rest—and all this is only what happens in the morning, and there is almost as large an attendance for the journey to evening service, after tea. Tea on Sunday, moreover, is particularly memorable; for the party would not get home again till rather late—dinner was consequently always " supper " on Sunday, in name if not in character—and this required, in Mrs. Chapman's view, that they should be fortified in advance with special precautions. Tea on Sunday was a feast, magnificently spread out in the dining-room, and the children " came down " ; and I like to remember that nobody could permit the good tradition to drop, even when its reason came to an end. Evening church, in our time, meant only the little walk to the village; but the grand Sunday tea remained unchanged, a relic of the legend of St. Giles.

We should glance with some pride, accordingly, at the handsome great tower, capped with its diminutive belfry, while the carriage skirted the enclosure of the graveyard. The parish of St. Giles is near the edge of the city (or it was), and the streets are gentlemanly and quiet and Georgian. Such is my impression; but I know there was plenty of scope, around and out of sight, for our grandfather's missionary zeal. He and his wife had laboured there abundantly and had left durable monuments of their care. The very church itself was one of these; for when they took the parish in hand, in the distant past, they found that a part of it had been allowed to tumble into a sad state of ruin, and the first necessity was to repair it and make it seemly for worship. So bad was its state that it had to be closed altogether for a good many months, while the work was in progress—and what was to be done meanwhile? Grandfather used to tell the story with spirit; the rector of a neighbouring parish, a small parish with a big church, had come forward with an offer. " See now," said the rector, " you've got there a bowtiful congregation and no church "—so grandfather reported the scene—" and here have I got a bowtiful church and no congregation; bring you your congregation then, and put them in my church, and we shall manage very well." So it was arranged; and when St. Giles's church was at last in order grandfather led his flock thither again, with all thanks to the neighbouring rector for his help in a difficulty. I always had a pleasant impression of the incident, and I should not fail to recall it as we waved our salute to St. Giles.

We should very soon reach the country and the high-road to Earlham; but the last outskirts of the city give me several pictures that I must not forget. It is certain, for example, that we should stop at English's, the chemist, which was a kind of clearing-house for goods and parcels directed to Earlham. English's was about the last shop you passed on the way out; hence its convenience for our purpose. When you went shopping in Norwich you had only to say " Send the parcel to English's "; whoever was driving out would be sure to stop there and clear the daily accumulation. At a sign from the coachman, as the carriage drew up, the accommodating Mr. English hurried out with a miscellaneous armful. That accomplished, I begin to find my pictures grow a little confused; for change was always at work in this quarter, and from one year to another buildings disappeared and sprang up in puzzling succession. Quite clear, however, is the vista of Chapel Field Road, striking off obliquely to the left along the line of the old city-wall; a solid stretch of the wall itself is to be seen in the back-gardens of the houses there, and grandmother used to tell us how the city-fathers in their vandalism had once started to pull down the " poor old wall " from end to end, but had been defeated at last in Chapel Field Road by its ancient toughness, and had desisted, leaving the relic we could still see triumphant. This was an image we enjoyed; we took sides with the wall against the stupid fury of modernity. I wish I could see Unthank Road as clearly; Unthank Road seems to have fallen below the strong effect of its name, which is all I retain of it. West Pottergate Street is another fine phrase that abides with me, but hardly more than a phrase.

In the very early days of my memory there was a building, near the limit of the city, which it was hard to pass with composure. It was the prison—such a terrific old place of black gates and bulging towers and high blind walls. A shudder seizes me; but mercifully the prison was soon to disappear, and very slowly another building arose in its place, so slowly that I think we followed its growth through many years. This was a large and splendid church, scrupulously Gothic, with curious rungs or handles attached to it—as though for the grasp of a giant bending over the pile to lift it bodily in the air; " flying buttresses " they were, I was told. It was not an ordinary church, it was a Roman Catholic Cathedral; and I looked at it, I well remember, with a shade of mute and mournful regret, puzzled and interested, wondering at so vast a monument of perversity and yet compelled to admire its insolence. But we scarcely spoke of it, the exotic upstart—we looked and passed; it could by no manner of means be regarded as part of *our* Norwich, and on the whole we ignored its intrusion. And very soon after it had been left behind we were out in the country and were mounting the long slope of Earlham Rise, past the gate and the straight avenue of the city cemetery, past a house or two and a farm and a few cottages; and presently it was time to be staring ahead for the first sight of home.

It began as a black wooden paling and a narrow belt of trees that ran beside the road on the left. The paling stretched far and far ahead, bordering the road, and in the distance you discerned where the black line was broken by a speck of white. I have never thought of that white speck without a quickening surge of excitement; for it was the gate, the white gate of the park, the end of our journey, descried in the distance by a child to whom the return to Earlham was the fulfilment of romance. It never failed; as the speck grew bigger and bigger I always knew that it satisfied my need, that it opened the way to what I wanted. And I can still detect a twinge of something like surprise, when we reach the gate at last and the carriage turns in and bowls along the drive—surprise that it should be so easy, after all, to penetrate into the heart of poetry. You look forward to it for ever so long beforehand, you wait and wonder and watch; and when the moment arrives so much seems to depend on it, the crisis has grown so big—and after all the carriage sweeps round and turns in at the gate quite naturally, and nobody thinks it strange, and the coachman on the box is only doing what he does every day of his life. I feel it distinctly as a twinge or tweak of oddity; but there is small time to weigh these grains of sensation at such a climax.

207

7

As the days slip forward I become aware that the
Sunday approaching has been fixed for our " harvest thanksgiving." To the children the festival
was always welcome; it was celebrated in Earlham
church, on some Sunday morning of September;
and it was rather a splendid occasion in itself, but
it was still more notable for the preparations it
demanded in advance. We plunged into them at an
early hour, on the morning before the appointed
day; other engagements all gave place—our help
was required, at least it was tolerated, in the
business of " decorating the church." Does it
sound a little tame? We certainly didn't find it so;
and when I now arrive in thought at the churchyard
gate, and climb the steep path to the porch, and
note that a stack of flowers and fruits and vegetables
has already been piled there for our use, I am inspired again with a certain stir of importance that
I should be sorry to have missed.

Our grandfather, I suppose, yielded to a popular
demand—for he was inclined to mislike these
celebrations. It is undeniable, you see, that in some
years the harvest is poor and thin; and are you
prepared to weigh the heartiness of your thanksgiving against the particular store of the season,
such as it may be? Will you presume to decide,
from year to year, whether the harvest has sur-
passed or fallen short of your just expectation,
whether it is richer or poorer than you deserve?
Not thus will a really grateful and humble soul be
willing to bargain and calculate. He will give

thanks at all hours and seasons for immeasurable mercies, he will bow his head to chastisement which must still be merciful; but to make a yearly practice of jubilantly singing " We plough the fields and scatter " on a particular Sunday—it is as much as to assume a recurring right to a plentiful harvest. So our grandfather argued—most reasonably, it seems to me. But he was never one to force an argument harshly; for even his strongest convictions, reaching far down into his character, found nowhere in him the strain of tyranny that is always so ready to turn a strong conviction to its own account. He believed, but his belief could never be seized upon and made use of by any lurking love of power, for he had none in any corner of his mind. He could not tyrannize, even in the smallest things; and so we had our harvest thanksgiving and made the most of it.

And to begin with the church must be decorated, and I perfectly understand the charm of helping or hindering that amusing process. The place where habitually one has to sit still and look on is the place where one always dreams of being allowed to play freely—it is natural enough. There were certain horrible little villa-gardens, with twisting walks and terrace-steps, which we could see from the train on the journey to London; and even the garden of Earlham hardly seemed a more alluring playground than these—to this day I look out for them to see if they still exist, still tempting the imagination. And the inside of a church, where every inch has been explored a hundred times by wandering eyes, is the place of all others in which

one would like to roam at ease and play the games
for which it is so well adapted. Pews and pulpit
and reading-desk, the chancel-screen, the gallery
under the tower, I knew them all as well as I knew
the nursery at home; and I could lose myself in the
fancy of being given the run of the church, some
week-day, and of setting up a shop for groceries in
one of the pews, climbing into the pulpit for a look-
out or addressing a mob from the gallery. I should
highly value, therefore, the right of entry into a
church at a time when there is freedom of movement, when I have the chance of investigating the
recesses that are hidden from my fixed post on
Sunday morning; and under colour of helping the
young ladies of the parish with their garlands and
festoons I can make some interesting researches of
my own.

Not indeed that the special business of the hour
is without its own appeal; I thoroughly enjoyed it,
I had my own view on the way in which the apples
should be piled about the font, the pumpkins
(relieved with asparagus-plumes) balanced on the
window-ledges and the bunches of scarlet dahlias
disposed upon the screen. The young ladies
worked brightly and sociably; I don't exactly
know who they were, but an impression of flushed
faces and loose hair remains with me, as well as a
distinct idea that one of them was the " beauty "
of the party—I had heard her so described, and you
could tell which she was by her superior manner of
keeping herself cool and aloof, while the others
grovelled among the apples and hoisted the pumpkins to their appointed places. By degrees we

contrived to smother the little church from end to end, it seems to me, with the spoils of the year; I particularly remember the two miniature sheaves or stooks of corn, tied with an artful touch of realism, that we placed in the embrasure of the tiny east window, over the ten commandments, with a mound of tomatoes between them. And I also remember very vividly indeed how the young ladies, as the morning wore on, lost some of their bright good-will, seemed disinclined for exertion, grew a little short and sharp with each other—a real bit of experience for me, I somehow felt, and a glimpse of curious life. I carefully took it in, and actually it represented, I believe, a discovery; for though the storms and squabbles of the nursery were of course familiar, the sight of grown-up people distinctly out of temper among themselves and on their own ground was new to me, I really think. Such an impression enlarged one's horizon, even if it damped the fun of the moment; and I had another revelation when our grandmother dropped in upon the scene, with her happy voice of greeting and congratulation, and immediately the young ladies were bright and good again, dissembling their breeze of ill-humour—one could easily see they were a little ashamed of it and felt a trifle awkward, and this too was a new light on the world. But I was far from blaming the poor things for their irritation; the beauty had been quite exasperating.

8

The north door of the little transept, standing open, would tempt one into the shadow of the

EARLHAM

churchyard. The low side of an old plastered house abuts on it in this quarter; square windows look out upon the graveyard, the yellowish wall catches the sunshine and lights up the northern shadow of the church. The house, I suppose, had once been the vicarage; but long ago the two small parishes, Earlham and Colney, had been united in one cure, and the vicarage had become The Lodge. That was the house in which our grandmother had lived in those early years of her far-away first marriage, when Uncle Joseph John, with his succession of wives and his fine old sister, was still serenely studying and meditating up at the Hall. Our young grandmother, walking thither with her husband to join him in a quiet stroll, may often have found him at work upon his manuscript; he would sit by the window of his small study—the school-room of our day—pondering his argument, polishing his phrase, forgetting the flight of the hours. He wrote several books, and after his death they were collected in a uniform edition; they stood on a shelf at Earlham, leather-bound and gilt, untouched for the rest of time. To his fresh young niece, when she came strolling up through the garden on the arm of her husband and looked in at the study-window, he would present a picture of wisdom and piety that had all her veneration; no doubt she listened with the deepest respect when he spoke of his manuscript and indicated the nature of the work, I dare say she even tried to read it when it was published. She intensely felt the privilege of associating with such a Christian and such a thinker; she would do her best to profit by

212

the opportunity, she would embark upon a course of serious reading, she would begin to fill a copy-book with notes on the history of the early church. Somehow the notes gave out after a page or two, and I am sure that in after years she could not have told us the name of any of Uncle Joseph John's collected volumes. But I hope the grave-eyed author had an inkling, when he looked up from his desk and met her bright admiring gaze, of the freedom and the sparkle of her genius compared with the dead weight of solemnity that was loading his page upon the evidential value of the story of Genesis regarded in the light of—enough, let the page lie forgotten, embalmed in the fragrance of our grandmother's respect for it.

She was a girl, still under twenty, and her husband was a good many years older and almost an invalid; and Earlham in those years was rather an elderly place for her, no doubt. The gay youth of its big family was long past; there were no more scarlet habits or purple boots to be seen at Earlham in the days when Joseph John was writing his books in the school-room, reconciling old faiths and new sciences. When his nephew brought our young grandmother to live at the Lodge, she might indeed consider herself privileged to join a circle that was at once so good and so wise—but is it possible that she ever felt a little lonely there, among these elderly ensamples of worth? If she did, I could believe that she never knew it herself, never doubted that her youth was entirely glad and eager to admire, to venerate, to follow the guidance of saintly age; and presently she had her own young children about her, and she was a matron of twenty among the responsibilities of life. She took up the tradition of Earlham and renewed it, as I have described, and that tradition had never become sombre or dull— it could never be that, with Aunt Catherine still at hand, and Aunt Cunningham descending with her sketch-books on a visit from Lowestoft, and old Samuel, their London brother, rumbling up from time to time in his ponderous silk-lined chariot. The old people were charming, their blitheness was unquenched; but still they *were* old by this time— for her at least they were old—and when I think of the young girl in their midst I can't help feeling that her opportunities of admiring and reverencing her elders were even excessive. From her childhood in the Cathedral Close, from the chatter of her sisters and the romantic elegance of her mother, she came straight into this circle of notable and substantial old people; and in her simplicity and her gratitude she could only begin to look up to them, continue to watch and wait upon their example—until a new generation was already about her, and she was herself the vessel of the old tradition.

Yet I hardly know—a nature like hers can spend itself in devotion, can surrender itself unconditionally, and at the same time always remain more independent and more original and more buoyant than another; our grandmother, young or old, must always have been herself. If I could now catch sight of her in her youth—say at such a moment as I have imagined, when she walked under the trees on the arm of her husband and glanced in at the window upon the quiet old man over his books—surely I should know her at once as we knew her fifty years after. In her youth she would sweep her voluminous skirt over the grass and hold her head up like a picture, as ever in her old age; and to the end of her life her quick clear spontaneity was the same as ever in her girlhood. She was grave and she was gay according to her own native law; all the influences of her reverend elders could not weight her youth unduly or fasten maturity upon her prematurely—because from the beginning she was herself, with a nature that unfolded and bloomed like a flower. In those days, therefore, when she lived at the Lodge and was treated by the circle of Earlham ever so affectionately, but still with an implication that a married woman of seventeen is well in the midst of the seriousness of life—in those days her genius already played easily, with its rightful freedom, and we have only to wish that her elders recognized and admired it properly. Most of them did for certain, especially Aunt Catherine; and if I have a lingering doubt about old Joseph John it probably does him injustice. When, leaving his desk, he paced the lawn with his nephew's young wife, I dare say his look brightened and twinkled through the smooth, too smoothly christian serenity that I always thought it wore in his portrait. I may wrong him in supposing that he held forth to her about his treatise on the fall of man; perhaps he recalled and described to her his encounter with the young fisherman down by the bridge, and the visit afterwards paid him by Lavengro.

9

The Lodge, embowered in great trees, looked out
upon the churchyard with its side-windows. Behind
and below it, towards the river, was the Farm, and
we might stray out through the ducks and the
turkeys to the water-meadows, where the shallow
stream, not here navigable, tinkled and bubbled
over a gravelly bed. But no, I take the road to
Colney, the high road that has arrived at Earlham
from Norwich and now proceeds over the bridge
towards the rising ground beyond. Earlham village
was hardly a village at all—the church, the Lodge,
the Farm, one small row of cottages, nothing more;
and then the road lifted itself gently over the solid
arch of the bridge and entered the parish of Colney.
It is worth while to pause upon the bridge, though,
partly to hang over the flat-topped parapet and
stare into the blackness of the pool, partly to note
the round cutting through the trees, leading to one
of the drawing-room windows up at the house—you
remember the drawing-room window-seat, where
the child sat and listened to the story of the blazing
house, and how one saw the view of the bridge from
it, neatly set in a round frame of greenery. From
the bridge one reverses the view, and I should not
pass on without dwelling upon the fact for a moment.

Then we wander on towards Colney (be sure to
call it Co'ney), which is upon higher ground and
is rather more of a village than Earlham. There
were scattered old cottages, red and grey, with
vines and pear-trees trained about their windows,
and presently a big farm to the left of the road; but

especially there was the church-tower, soon in sight, which was a curiosity we were proud of. It is one of those round towers of flint, smooth and bare, that are not very uncommon in East Anglia, I know; but to our eyes it was rare and strange, and it gave character to a village that otherwise hadn't really very much. And it was not only the tower— the church within had a singular interest, to my mind, in the days I speak of. It was all furnished with high square pews, like rows of little roofless houses; I had never seen anything of the sort elsewhere, and I believed them peculiar to Colney church. You enter into your queer small house and shut the front-door—it is charming; the world is completely cut off by the high walls, you see nothing above them but the rafters of the church-roof and the top of the chancel-arch. If only I could be left to myself in such a place, I could live a life there that would satisfy many dreams; a whole street of private houses, each with its own front-door and its four solid walls—it is almost cruel how they stand there waiting to be used, to be drawn into a sequence of adventure that is absolutely denied to me. There was no chance that Colney church would ever be placed at my disposal for the kind of life I could see myself leading there; it was useless to think of it.

What happened instead, though it began well, turned very soon to a dreary affair. The high pew was empty within, save for a few red hassocks and a bench that ran round three sides of the square; and by the time the Sunday morning party has entered in and shut the door and taken their seats

on the bench, you may say that the entertainment
of the occasion is over. It is all very well to admire
the privacy and seclusion of your retreat, once the
front-door is shut and latched; but I can't tell you
how soon the hardness of the bench and the short-
ness of one's legs and the blankness of the four walls
—how soon, in fact, the case becomes intolerable.
The voice of the minister falls and rises, the clerk
mouths out the responses with the low buzz of the
congregation behind him, the harmonium, with that
strange mewing voice that I know so well, sets up
the tune of "Rockingham"—and all unseen,
hidden from sight behind the dull wooden walls;
and it really seems impossible to last out the hour
of the service with nothing to look at. So I should
say, so indeed I felt it; and yet I find that once
at any rate, during a session in the high pew at
Colney church, there fell a flash, there washed over
me a wave of sweetness, which was wonderful just
because it came so unexpectedly out of the unseen.
I remember perfectly how the enclosure in which
we sat appeared to contain and to circumscribe all
the resources of the hour; the music and the voices
without, since I could not see what was happening,
were removed from my circle of experience—I
could do nothing with them. And as for the
resources at hand, the hassocks and the prayer-
books, the graining of the wooden walls, the features
and attitudes of my two or three companions, these
I had soon exhausted, and my world for the hour
before me looked empty indeed. I had no thought
of anything entering it, piercing a way into my life,
from the region without, where the buzzing and

218

droning of the service went forward; and then suddenly a hymn was started, not Rockingham this time, which for some reason or other rolled over and invaded me as though it sought me out on purpose. It seemed to be sung for me—I accepted it at once; I shall never forget how the first phrase of the tune settled into my brain as though taking possession of its own. It was nothing new, it was an old tune we had heard and sung a hundred times; but it became entirely new at that moment and always afterwards remained so. " Our blest Redeemer, ere he breathed—his Ten-der last farewell ": it was only that—and I have never heard or thought of it since then without standing on a footstool in a high pew, between two grown-up companions, with the rafters of Colney church overhead.

10

Yet the village of Colney always seemed to me slightly foreign and strange. It lay upon the very limit of our ordinary beat; our straggling walks took us no further out into the world in that quarter, as it happened. The road ran on, but so much had always delayed us by the way, in a short mile or so, that it was time to turn round and go home; beyond Colney was the unknown, and Colney itself, I felt, was never completely mine. One's normal range, in fact, is not very wide by any measure, so long as a morning's walk is the kind of progress that I closely connect with the Colney road. I should set forth on that walk quite briskly, stepping out by the side of our companion in charge and

easily breaking into a trot now and then to maintain
our pace. We should positively scud down the
drive and through the village and over the bridge,
devouring the way; and yet we seem to have gone
no distance at all before I find myself adrift,
detached from the party, staring after them over an
increasing interval. It was natural to pause by the
bridge, as I have explained; and from that moment
onwards our brisk and business-like expedition
begins to fall to pieces. The interval over which
I must overtake the party is impossible; strive as I
may, it never grows less. If I stop for an instant
they are almost out of sight, and the hard wail of my
voice is still in my ears—" Wait for Meeeee!"

So it is not surprising that we never saw much of
the outland country beyond Colney. That was a
region that was lighted in my imagination by little
but the names, the glorious names of the villages,
which flashed out casually in the conversation of
our uncles and grandparents. I have named some
of them; but did I mention Bawburgh, which we
speak of as " Baber "?—I particularly liked the
look of it on a sign-post. On days of early September, that were still like high August, we might
see our uncles drive forth in the dog-cart from
Earlham with guns, with leather patches on their
shoulders, with caps that were peaked both fore
and aft and tied up at the top—drive forth to
shooting-parties in that world of the unknown, from
which they returned with flights of jest and anecdote finer than ever. I had the strongest impression
of the free manly life of dog-carts and gun-cases
and jovial fellowship at such times—life that sent

out a tumultuous surge all round it, till even the small cockle-shell of my own being, infinitely far from the centre, began to jump beneath me. The shooting-parties were wildly beyond our ken, and the uttermost reverberation of them was quite enough for me; but I know there were moments when I really was a little ashamed of the mild triviality of our own occupations, and still more ashamed of being so well content with them.

The world of men, however, which had little need for me when it shot, opened to us most interestingly at certain other times. They shoot a great deal in September, especially in Norfolk; but particularly in Norfolk they do more—they go on the Broads. They disappear for days and weeks together; and we at home, when we are asked what they are doing, reply simply that they are " on the Broads." What does it mean? For a long while, though the phrase was very familiar to me, I hadn't the least idea what it meant; the phrase sufficed. Earlham does not lie in the region of the Broads; but there came a day when at last we made the excursion thither, and saw for ourselves how life is lived on them. We visited a party of young men who were sketchily keeping house in a beautiful ship; we spent some brilliant hours with them on the open waters of Wroxham or Ranworth—and that was life on the Broads. There were many such days, first and last, days of dazzling suns and flapping sails and popping corks—so the impression returns to me. The reed-beds and the vast pale sky and the long level lines of the green shore were delicious as the blaze of the waters gradually faded; we made our way into some staithe or winding creek; we scrambled to land and found flowering bulrushes and loaded ourselves with spoils for the journey home. At the end of such a day, sleepily nodding in the train that took us back to Norwich, I could feel replete with large experience. I didn't envy the young men in their ship—far from it; the path of prudence took one home in the train, at the end of the day, by the time when the sense of adventure began to droop, as it will, with the failing light. But I had no reason to envy them, for I carried my adventure away with me, safely stored, and could always fall back on it when I would. When you have once spent a day at Wroxham with a party of competent and masterful young men, nothing can ever remove it from your past; you are one who has " been on the Broads," and I seem to remember that you allow no one to forget it.

The day when we visited the Decoy—that was rather different; for the Decoy was on an outlying lake, and we were taken there by a party that was neither manly nor mature. I see a boat-full of friends and cousins, not at all elderly, with whom we paddle out upon a long stretch of water surrounded by a wooded shore. At the far end of the lake, out of sight, lies the Decoy, whatever you may understand by that. I don't know what I expected to see, but I was very anxious to see it; and we paddled away down the lake and sidled along the shadowy bank. And very memorable it was that at a certain point we ran into a small grove of rushes, growing in the water, and these were *scented* rushes, deliciously odorous and aromatic, such as I had never met with before but once—need I say where and when? It was in the Fifth Square, which as you know was mostly water; Alice was rowing the boat, the sheep was sitting in the stern with her preposterous knitting; and Alice plucked up the rushes by handfuls, just as we did, and piled them on the floor of the boat. I was disappointed to find that they didn't fade any faster than you would expect, but otherwise they were the true scented rushes of the Looking-glass, growing in real life. I have always liked to recall them, more especially as the Decoy didn't really satisfy me after all, when we reached it at last. It is strange and mysterious indeed—the large netted archway that spans the mouth of the creek, gradually narrowing as the creek curves away from the entrance; so that you sail in unsuspectingly and follow the curve and find yourself caught in a bag, so to speak, at the end of it. It is strange—but it is empty and silent, or it was on that day, and I couldn't very well understand the system of its working, when it is worked. There is a mazy contrivance of reed-fences, along the edge of the creek, among which a trained dog dashes and barks to drive the ducks in to their doom; it was all explained to us, explained too much, and I soon got lost. I was more at home in the Fifth Square, across which we presently returned.

II

But these excursions into the outer world were special and exceptional, and I soon get back to the Colney road and the long straggle of the way home.

The interest of a walk, I always find, is over when
it is time to turn round and retrace one's steps;
from that moment I am solely given up to the effort
of progress, trying to reduce the everlasting interval
between myself and the rest of the party. Nothing
happens, nothing relieves the mechanical plod of
the journey; that mile or so of plain road between
Colney village and Earlham bridge is like a hundred.
Nothing happens—but I do remember, it is true,
the sight of our grandfather's tall black figure issuing from a cottage-door by the wayside, and how he
smiled at us with his "How do you do, sir—how
do you do, miss," humorously formal, and marched
away down the road with the steady rhythm of his
big boots. He had been making a parochial round,
no doubt; and I reflect that I never happened to
see him, as I saw our grandmother so often, talking
and ministering to the old souls of the parish. He
had dropped in for a visit and a chat in the course
of his round; but I can't picture the interview—
evidently his way must have been quite different
from grandmother's lyrical, tuneful, clear-ringing
intimacy. When his voice was raised in prayer, as I
have said, all barriers seemed to be broken down,
his heart was laid bare. But in intercourse with
the world he spoke from behind a veil of reserve—
light and grey and soft, never hiding the shine of his
benevolence, only muffling and muting his tone just
a little; and I wonder what he talked to Mrs. Giles
about, when he dropped in for a morning call.

"Master'll be home before us—he walk so fast."
The words, falling on my ear in a well-known voice,
remind me that the companions of our walk *had*

waited for me and that I was clinging to the kindly arm of one of them when we sighted our grandfather. By the household of Earlham he was always spoken of as " Master," and grandmother as " Mistress "; and in the speech of all the household there were agreeable touches of the Norfolk manner, native to each one of them. " He walk so fast—he never dawdle," says our dear and fond companion (she was grandmother's maid in those days); and we forgot to loiter and lag, I dare say, in the ready charm of her conversation. Everybody at Earlham talked well, and with this particular friend I sometimes thought that I too was quite at my best. We chatted lightly, with swift retorts and rejoinders in excellent style; we kept up an easy give-and-take, never flagging on either side. There were exquisite jokes that dated from the far past and that sprang up unfailingly from year to year—jokes that leaped to life again at a word, an allusion, with the rare property (since lost to such things) of growing funnier by simple repetition. One or two of them could beguile that endless journey home; but whatever pace we might make we should certainly be left far behind by grandfather's mile-devouring tramp.

I can't picture his call upon Mrs. Giles—for he had no vestige of the conventional brightness and heartiness of the minister among the poor of his parish; he had no professional manner or trick to fall back upon in the routine of his office. He never looked like a country parson walking through his village; he looked like a tall grave scholar, a clerical don perhaps, tramping out for his daily hour of exercise and fresh air. You would expect

the incumbent of a parish to seem more prepared
for the fray, more equipped for conquest, shining
with the assurance of his mission, issuing forth in
the morning to enter the lives of others for their
good; such at least is the image that occurs to me
when I notice the very different style of our grandfather. So far from assuming a right and a duty to
lay hold of the lives of his neighbours, even in the
name of charity, he appeared to pause diffidently
and civilly, refusing to take any such liberty unin-
vited. Missionary zeal is a fine flame, but it does
not abolish the law of simple good manners; and
that law will make one hesitate, I should hope,
before encroaching as of right upon the privacy of
another. Our grandfather, I think, treated his
parishioners exactly as he would treat a guest under
his roof and at his table—they had a like claim for a
courteous consideration of their prejudices, their
shortcomings. It is impossible to see him intruding
into the affairs of his flock with free familiarity,
just because he happened to be their pastor. To
grandmother these scruples were quite unknown;
but she too made nothing of any difference between
the guest at Earlham and Mrs. Giles in her cottage
at Colney. She never paused upon any threshold;
she entered in, and the word of greeting, of sympathy, of advice—and of reproof, if so it chanced—
sprang straight from her heart. But neither did
she, any more than he, set out with a mission to do
good; she did what she could not help doing—good
everywhere.

I very much doubt, therefore, whether grandfather had really taken the old woman at Colney

to task for her delinquencies—supposing she had
laid herself open to reproach. He had probably sat
with her and talked of the weather and her rheuma-
tism and her grandchildren, without so much as
touching upon the question of her obstinate refusal
to come to church more regularly. But then there
was another side to the manner of his ministration,
and I am sure it was not often or for long that that
side was ever obscured. He could not reprove or
find fault, and perhaps he could not mix intimately
with the world on any common terms; but in
prayer he was transformed, and when he prayed
there was no separation between himself and his
companions. He was transformed—but it was
rather as though he then came to his own, passed
on to his own ground, leaving behind him the region
where true intercourse is hampered by accident and
trivial difficulties. Prayer seemed his natural voice,
and the beautiful freedom of its tone was enhanced
by the contrast with its veiled and dusky shynesses
at other times. I have witnessed the change so
often; it happened so often and so simply that in
some small gathering of his family, when we sat
sociably in the evening and he listened to the light
talk in kindly silence—it happened so familiarly
that before we dispersed he would kneel, and we
with him, while he spoke at last and uttered the
abundance of his heart. None of us, not the
youngest, had ever the sense that he was moved to
do so as our confessor, our mentor, conscious of a
charge and a responsibility towards us; he never
prayed because it was good for us to hear him. He
prayed because in that communion he contemplated

227

beauty, was in the presence of the summit of all desire—and he, prayed, forgetful of himself, yet mindful of the companionship of all those who love and believe in beauty. I so express it, recalling the memory from many years ago, though of course these are not the words he would have used himself; I speak of beauty and of desire, where he would have spoken of God and of the soul's repose upon her maker, because even the youngest of us who listened to him may well have then learned, without discovering the knowledge till long afterwards, the manifest oneness of all the objects of our adoration. Our grandfather, I see, lived daily and hourly with the perfection of beauty in his mind and heart, like a poet—and like a poet whose fire is never chilled. He knew familiarly the lonely raptures of an artist; they supported him always and everywhere, not only in the few fortunate moments that an artist has mostly to be contented with.

And they were *not* lonely, what is more; his joy reached outward, into the world around him, and grew upon the sense of the widening commonalty of the faith. It was in the trivial businesses of life, and only there, that he might seem solitary, aloof from our sociable clatter; it was not so, far from it, when he knelt and surrendered himself to the vision of power and love. There was nothing jealous, nothing secluded or remote, in the spirit of his worship; it broadened out to embrace the company of all the faithful, millions strong, who join their voices in thanksgiving. There are many, I suppose, to whom the act of adoration is always a matter of the innermost chamber, sealed and guarded, deaf and blind to the world without; there are many of these, not poets only, but saints in all ages. And really I could believe that this is the one fundamental distinction in humanity, the one irresoluble difference between soul and soul— that some of us adore in solitude, some in the congregation of our kind. To the man I speak of, at any rate, the fellowship of prayer and praise was intensely real, profoundly inspiring and uplifting; and in a man whose outer habit was so quietly toned and subdued, who moved through the world with so little insistence or gesture or obtrusive demand—in such a man this high and appealing accent of spiritual brotherhood was memorably impressive, I know well.

12

Sunday morning at last—a morning not unwelcome at Earlham, but a morning that always began, I fear, with trouble; for one is met, on getting out of bed, with the horror of " clean things," laid out for the Sunday toilet. I can't describe my hostility towards the starched and crackling tissues in which I must clothe myself on Sunday; and as for the loathsome clinging and tickling of clean stockings, clean underwear, week by week it rouses me to a passion of protest that I can't even try to control. It is a horrid business; but I am bound to say the worst is soon over, and it is easily forgotten before it is time to set out for the walk to church. Every hour at Earlham had pleasing peculiarities on Sunday; for example after prayers (which were much shorter than usual) came the question of the hymns

229

for morning and evening service, and we could help grandmother in making a note of the numbers chosen and of the tunes to which they were to be sung. The hymn chosen was "common measure," she said, or "long measure," and this tune or that (she knew them by name) would fit it rightly. At Earlham they didn't use our familiar "Ancient and Modern," I think because it was held to be rather priestly and Roman; they used a book which grandmother referred to as "Bickersteth," and if the appointed tunes were outside our range, she knew others of the due measure that met the case. So that was settled, and by half past ten the children were ready and waiting upon the cool north steps of the front door.

Earlham in the morning, Colney in the evening, and the opposite on alternate Sundays—that was the rule; and the morning of harvest thanksgiving would certainly fall on the turn for Earlham. So the walk is nothing, merely down the park to the end of the drive; and small parties of the household gradually muster and set forth through the freshness of the lime-avenue. We walked decorously, feeling very new and clean, hugging our prayer-books; and I remember, by the way, how amusing it was to discover that the neat little volume carried by one of our uncles was really a small French dictionary—he couldn't find the right book, he had picked another of appropriate size at random. It seemed a stroke of wit, and I enjoyed it; he gravely folded the thing under his arm and marched down the drive. We reached the road, we passed into the churchyard and up the path to the porch; and here through the open door came familiar sounds from within—so familiar that they bring me suddenly to a pause, at this late day, as they come back to me out of the long silence. I had quite forgotten that grandmother was always ahead of us on these occasions; she started early, she was already there when we arrived—because there were a few minutes of choir-practice before the service; and it was the cheerful noise of the choir-practice that now pealed out to meet us. I had strangely forgotten it; but the exact ring of the voices, with the breathless snatches and gusts of the harmonium behind them, is restored to me again as I mount the churchyard-path and turn in at the door.

Choir-practice, we called it; but you are not to picture any such scene as the word suggests to you. There were no vain forms and shows in Earlham church, no pomp of little boys in surplices, nothing of that kind. There was only our renowned Eliza, with the remarkable organ of her voice—only she and two or three lesser lights who gathered about her in the gallery under the tower; that was all the choir there was, and they had little enough to practice, merely two or three old-established hymn-tunes out of "Bickersteth." But they sang them over before the service, by way of precaution, and grandmother took her place in the gallery and added her clear voice to the chorus. She was supposed to sit in the chancel, where she had her proper place in the chief corner, just within the old wooden screen; and she did sit there sometimes, when all seemed to be going well in the gallery and the hymns were well supported. But she ranged as she would,

231

and this morning at any rate her help would decidedly be needed among the high notes of " We plough the fields and scatter " ; there are passages in that tune, as you remember, that go shooting up to a pitch where most of our voices are strangled to a very thin shriek. " He sends ther snow in Win Ter ther warmth ter swell ther Grain "—our stream of song was reduced to a painful thread, compassing that phrase ; but grandmother soared over it like a bird and dropped softly and sweetly to the lower levels of " the breezes and the sunshine," where the roar of the congregation swelled out again in confidence.

Nor was Eliza ever known to quail before the steepest ascent. I can't say that she flew like a bird, but she strode onward and upward over the boulders of the melody without the least discomposure, never missing her step. She was the daughter of the under-coachman, conspicuous in the gallery with her handsome head and the far-away shine of her eyes ; and her voice was a marvel that impressed and affected me intensely. It was like a polished rod of song, straight and smooth, which she seemed to carry aloft in both hands, holding it high without a tremor ; and wherever we climbed and panted, there was Eliza before us, full in view, with the gleaming shaft of her voice to point the way. She was always in her place, absolutely to be relied on, and the pleasant little gentleman at the harmonium had only to follow her lead. He, I think, walked out from Norwich every Sunday to play the harmonium at the two services—a little mild-eyed, sandy-haired gentleman, gratefully un-

assuming, who seems to belong to a novel of
Dickens; he passed the interval between the
services up at the Hall, under the bountiful pro-
tection of Mrs. Chapman. Such, with three or four
vocalists of no particular note, was the company
that assembled in the gallery to practise the hymns,
and it was their final and triumphant assault upon
" We plough the fields " that echoed out into the
churchyard as we approached.

Full in front of us, on our entry, was the font—
the font with the diadem of pippins and marigolds
that we had designed and wrought for it the day
before. From thence the eye was caught to the
pumpkins on the window-sills, from thence again
to the frills of ripe wheat and dahlias upon the
carving of the screen, to the enormous bunch of
black grapes that hung from its middle archway,
and so forward to the sheaves of corn above the
communion-table. The effect was even richer than
I expected; we had laboured well, and everybody
was struck by the ingenuity of our art. The whole
church was filled with the sweetness of apples,
mellifluously mingled with the cool smell of antiquity that belonged to the building. Our pew was
in the chancel, to the right; and through the arcad-
ing of the screen, as through a window, I could
survey the gathering of the congregation. Our own
household bulked large in it, with Mrs. Chapman
very tight and trim in her best; they made a
familiar island among the village faces. It didn't
take long for the seats to fill, and by this time a
spirited prelude or " voluntary " (whatever that
may be) was taxing the last breath of the

harmonium. The Major (whom I have not yet introduced) took his place with dignity in the chancel-pew opposite to ours, and we were ready to begin.

13

It was like nothing else that I have ever seen or heard. It was very informal, but it was utterly dignified; it was very plain, but it was strangely poetic; it was very cheerful and brisk, but it had none of that resolute good humour, that hand-rubbing hospitality, those teeth-clenching high spirits, with which some have tried to soften the shock and chill of unaccustomed piety. Grandfather towered in his reading-desk above the tiny assembly—not screened away in the chancel, but full in the midst, commanding the little toy-nave of the church; he lifted up his eyes benignly and mildly, with a look that seemed to draw his flock after him, not magisterially directing or urging it. He welcomed his people indeed, but he carried them above the level of common and personal things—how can I express it?—he addressed them as christian souls; and he arrogated nothing to himself, no priestly right of dictation, no inquisitorial claim—he simply showed the way and gazed forward and spoke for the equal company that followed him. And while he read and preached with so little of the assumption of his office, he was just as far from condescending in kindness to the simplicity of his hearers; he did not unbend, he did not doff his dignity, to put us at our ease and make us comfortable after the strain of getting to church.

234

OUTSIDE AND BEYOND

All that rubbish was unheard-of at Earlham; sincerity was simple, simplicity was sincere, in the agreeable scene that I wish I could describe as clearly as I now behold it.

The doors stood open, the windows were flung wide—grandmother saw to that; the southern airs fluttered in over our heads, where we sat in the chancel, and stirred the garlands upon the screen. On the wall opposite to me was a tablet with a long inscription, of the eighteenth century, which I read and re-read and knew by heart from the earliest days; and close at my right was the low rail of the communion-table, and the table itself, very plain with its red cloth and white linen. The small two-lighted east window contained the only painted glass of the church; it had been set there by our grandmother to the memory of her first husband, dead so long and long ago; and no vain images or figures appeared in it, nothing but a text or two, I think, surrounded by thick-coloured foliation. What next? Oddly enough, immediately over our heads, there was a big tablet on the wall with a long-winded Latin dedication to a gentleman of our own peculiar name; and what is more, if you lifted the mat in the aisle, just below the chancel-step, you discovered a stone in the floor with the legend "Entrance to the vault of Dr. Lubbock"; and I never knew anything of these old kinsmen of ours, or how they had found their way to Earlham church, but as kinsmen I claimed them, and it was agreeable to think that they bound us to the place with yet another tie. Our uncouth name is indigenous in Norfolk; I believe it is to be found on village

235

tomb-stones in many churchyards of the county; so we could doubly feel that we were returning to our own when we came again among the winding waters and the turnip-slopes and the oak-shaded lanes of the eastern land. And in Earlham church the very bones that lay mouldering beneath our feet were akin to us, we might reasonably think.

I cannot tell the degree of our cousinship with Dr. Lubbock in his vault; but I cling to him the more because our familiar old Gurneys had naturally left no traces of themselves in the parish church at their gates. If they died at Earlham they were buried at " Goat's "—a hard price, I should call it, to pay for the privilege of enrolment as a Friend. How could one submit to burial at Goat's, with all the poetry of Earlham church so near at hand? The Norwich meeting-house of the Friends was in Goat's Lane, and the young Gurneys in their purple and scarlet days, dragged thither twice every Sunday, had this opprobrious name for the place. There they must lie at last—there or in some other such crude and nude conventicle of their faith— while Dr. Lubbock might rest among the fore-fathers of the village, mingling his dust with the ages. A few of our Gurneys did, it is true, lapse into the bosom of the church as they grew older; but none of them fell to be buried or commemorated at Earlham—none of that big gay family over whom Aunt Catherine had presided for so long. Only with the generation that followed, when our grandmother became one of them, did they begin to find their rest in the churchyard of the village; and so it was that their name was missing from among the old inscriptions that I studied upon the chancel-wall and learned by heart. That one immediately opposite me was very queer and involved; it related to a member of the Earlham family of prehistoric and pre-Gurney days, and it told a long story about the burial of the gentleman elsewhere and his removal when the church was demolished—such a confusing rigmarole, even to one who had spelt it out again and again with eyes that peered through locked fingers, his head bowed in the attitude of prayer.

My mind has been wandering, as you see; I couldn't stop the roving of my gaze, as we knelt in our pew, though my face was decently buried in my hands and only a chink or two left open between my fingers. I had strayed far away from the open pages of my prayer-book, which lay on the little shelf between my elbows; but the voice of our grandfather recalls me as soon as we reach the antiphon of versicle and response in which we take our part. There was a curious interest in this, for grandfather had an easy way of his own with the more formal parts of the service. He took them at a swinging and rhythmical canter that always pleased me; he caught us up, he broke into the soft rumble of our responses before we had finished them, his voice was soaring into the next phrase while we were still busy with the last. I particularly liked this habit of his when we came to the psalms; it made them fly apace, which is not what they usually do when we say them verse by verse, in the form of a dialogue. In general, I think, the minister's share in the antiphon is unduly drawn out, with emphatic

237

intonations that we cannot imitate in our many-voiced response; we wait too long for our turn, and the two sides of the dialogue fall away from each other rather awkwardly. I found our grandfather's manner much more agreeable; not a moment was wasted, the psalm was reeled through its course in a spirited fashion, and from a plodding task it became quite an exhilarating outburst of sound and movement. It seemed perfectly natural that grandfather should hurry us forward and anticipate us as he did; that was his manner, his idiosyncrasy, whether he was reading at home or in church; he had no dressed-up, unwonted style that he assumed in public. His church was a fine old room, large enough for the gathering of the village, consecrated by its ancient associations—so he seemed to regard it, and not at all as a place to be essentially more reverenced, more formally honoured, than any other Christian habitation. Wherever we met for prayer was honourable ground, and there was no difference that he cared to mark between one day or one place and another.

Our Sunday assembly in church, therefore, was just like our daily session for prayers at home; the mood, the manner, the atmosphere were the same. It was enough, so far as I was concerned, to dissociate Earlham church entirely from any other place of worship that we knew—and there were two or three that we knew extremely well. It is remarkable to find yourself sincerely interested and pleased by the well-worn round of Sunday morning, to walk off to church at eleven o'clock with a gay hum of anticipation in your mind; I never had

such an experience anywhere else. The hour in
Earlham church was actually an hour of life, instead
of an hour in which you wait and wait for life to
begin again. I had no sense of being left out of the
proceedings, of looking on with a cold eye at an
affair that didn't belong to me; it was a family
party in which we shared alike, one and all—simply
because our grandfather at the reading-desk, our
grandmother in the gallery, were so serenely the
same as they were at home. Grandfather's serenity,
however, was tried and troubled one Sunday morning, I well remember; I can't tell, I doubt if I ever
knew, whether I really witnessed the scene, but it is
perfectly clear in my memory. He was in the
middle of his sermon, one morning, when a child
in the gallery was seized with a fit of coughing and
choking—which it couldn't stop, so that it spluttered
and hawked aloud, worse and worse, till everybody's
attention was disturbed and grandfather was forced
to intervene. He beckoned from the pulpit to the
child's mother and called out to her to take the
child away. You can imagine the little scene, the
note of vexation in the mild voice of the preacher,
the small scuffle of mother and child in the gallery.
But you must have heard it to hear again, as I do,
the clear ring of grandmother's quick exclamation,
her cry of reassurance to our grandfather—cheer-
fully pealing across the church from the gallery
where she had turned to help the embarrassed
mother. " It's all right, dear," she cried, looking
round from her ministration, and her voice flew
brightly across the hush of the assembly; " it's
all right now—I've given him a lozenge." That was

Earlham church. I don't believe I was there at the time, after all; but it matters little, I am certainly there now.

14

The lessons were read by the Major. He sat in the chancel-pew opposite ours, and when we settled down after the psalms he stood in his place and turned to the congregation, facing it through one of the windows of the screen. He rested his book upon the ledge before him and adjusted his eye-glasses so that they gripped, most strangely, the tip of his well-bridged nose. He was very old, I supposed, but he had a stately port; he was our neighbour at Earlham, living with his large family hard by the church. He wore his glasses in that interesting fashion so that he could look through them downward upon the open page, without bending his head; he read the lessons in measured and sonorous tones—and for me, listening to him now, the lesson is always the same, a chapter inseparably mingled with the sound of his voice. It is the story of Ahab's end, the battle of Ramoth-gilead; and if it cannot have been this chapter that fell to be read at harvest thanksgiving in September, it is this and no other that the Major reads when I sit and watch him now, wondering still at the odd balance of his glasses. It was their firm grip, perhaps, that gave a slightly nasal tone to his reading. I watched and listened with fascinated attention— a tribute certainly due to the reader himself and not to the far-off story of the battle, which only found its way into my mind because I could not help hanging absorbed upon the Major's utterance.

"So the king of Israel and Jehoshaphat the king of Judah went up to Ramoth-gilead." I knew the story very well—at least I knew how it ran, how the phrases followed upon each other, and I suppose I had a picture of some sort in my mind. But what can it have been? If it was a picture of ancient kings in a strange land it must have drawn me away from Earlham church on a Sunday morning —away from the presence of the Major, standing there erect in his corner, facing the congregation with eyes downcast upon his book. "But the king of Syria commanded his thirty and two captains that had rule over his chariots"—how can a child have listened with all ears to the words and not have dropped out of time, out of the moment, to follow the story through the heat of the day of battle in an unknown land? It is a battle that rages interminably under a blazing sky; it sways doubtfully—and everything hangs upon a chance, a bow drawn at a venture, a wounded man propped up in his chariot as the sun goes down; and at last the whole army knows what has happened, the proclamation runs round, the king of Israel is dead. He is defeated, he is dead and buried in Samaria, the dogs lick his blood when the chariot is washed in the pool; but he had been a great king, he had made an ivory house and built cities before he slept with his fathers. The story is soon told, and Ahaziah his son reigns in his stead; and yet it is as long as an epic, marching slowly and spaciously to its end. It drives a rift through centuries of darkness, showing the blaze and the confusion and the sudden hush and chill of bad news towards evening—a flash of old life that abolishes time.

It is a long way from Earlham church, you might think. A saga of eastern sheikhs, mustering their chariots and fighting and dying beyond Jordan, a tale of vaulting ambition and lying pride and insolence drowned in blood—there is not much here to remind me of an English summer morning, a red-cushioned chancel-pew and a child in a small white suit of Sunday clothes. And yet it is only with an effort that I can now read that story for what it is, for the merciless old saga, putting aside the swarm of friendly and homely memories that rise out of the page; and I see that the child in the starched white suit had never the least difficulty in reconciling the story with the life of Earlham. The battle of Ramoth-gilead worked in quite naturally; the tale was familiar, it belonged to the hour and it came to life again in the Major's evenly measured tones; Ahab and Jehoshaphat, so far from carrying me into the distance and the past, dropped into their places in the picture that included the Major, our uncle with his little French dictionary, Eliza in the gallery, the whole of the bare-headed or neatly bonneted congregation of Earlham village. There they all are together to this day—the chronicles of Israel have had strange fortunes. "And Ahaziah his son—reigned in his stead," declares the Major, sinking his voice upon the words, closing the Bible, removing his glasses. We all rise, I seize my open prayer-book and mount upon my footstool to join in the brisk give-and-take of the Te Deum.

15

On our last Sunday at Earlham, however, the last of the blissful summer holiday, things must fall out differently; I prefer to think that it was the turn of Earlham church in the evening. That is the picture I should wish to be left with when it is time to depart; and the time is upon us, the richest of the summer is over, the twilight begins to shut down with the first thin chill of autumn. We should certainly want to make the most of our last evening at Earlham; nothing should escape us, every moment should be of the best. Full of that determination I can loiter once more in the lime-avenue after tea, feeling the change that has come about there in one short month, the last of the summer. A drift of brown and yellow leaves upon the path, a damp wanness in the light of evening—one hardly notices the detail of such things, but they make all the difference to the mood of the hour and they start a new thrill in the romance of Earlham. Just here and now, on the eve of departure, you can see that the timeless, changeless Earlham of our few summer weeks is stirring and lapsing with the turn of the year; its life is proceeding, it begins to face toward the autumn days and nights—and I had felt till now that its life stood still and that its gorgeous dream of high summer was above the chances of the season. It is oddly moving to discover that the place is making its own plans for the coming months, that already it is intent upon things that will happen to it when we are gone. We have no part in its cold pale autumn,

243

and I might have forgotten what is in store for it; but on our last evening autumn is in the air, change is stealing into the golden ripeness of the garden.

The hours that were thus running out for us were keenly savoured, I am sure. We lingered about the lime-avenue, we strayed down the path towards the village, with senses alerter than ever to catch the peculiar voice and look and fragrance of the place. We demanded that everything should be right, should be exactly what it ought to be, for our last day of Earlham—the last till next time. It was easy to make sure of keeping it at the proper pitch; there was nothing in house or garden or park that could fail to reach the level of our supreme good will. I never went away without feeling that on this particular visit I had acquired rather more of Earlham, more of its rare and special virtue, than I ever had before; I could count up the new dis-coveries I had made and add them securely to the rest. They would be much in my mind as the sun sinks on our last evening, and I almost wonder that I am not more dejected by the thought of our imminent departure. But the fact is that the whole transaction of the visit to Earlham was exquisite to the very end, the end was even as good as the beginning. There was a certain form and manner of going away that was always observed; we could rely on it in advance, we could be confident that our farewell to the place would have its own accustomed interest. And I see that already the thought of the morrow was agreeably exciting, not depressing in the least; so that we rouse the pensive stillness and limpness of the September evening with a heightened bustle of enjoyment.

A journey is a journey after all, even when it takes you away from Earlham, and I welcomed a day of travel for its own sake. Not only the hours in the train, good as they were, but the flutter of preparation at one end, the disorder of unpacking and resettling at the other—it was all pleasure, not a minute of the day was wasted. Long before any one else the children would be ready to start; and the only trouble was the slight fret of anxiety, I remember it well, lest the elders of the party should take things too easily and be late. They always seemed to think there was more and more time for last words, after-thoughts, sudden searches for things overlooked—when we knew we ought to be off to catch the train. But there would still be plenty of time in hand when the children began to hover about the front door, hatted and booted, clasping some very particular object apiece that was too precious to be packed. There was ample time for a last dash into the garden, a visit to the sulkies or the weeping ash; yet as soon as we were out of the house there seemed to be no time at all, and I never was proof against the panic that sends one scurrying indoors again at a gallop—to find that the hand of the hall-clock is still almost exactly where it was, half an hour to the time of departure. But then came a very interesting episode. As we sit in the hall, on the big red seat by the gong, I see the study-door open and grandfather appear on the threshold; and with a humorous and mysterious look he beckons to us, silently

makes a little knowing sign which brings us quickly
across the floor and into his room. There the sun
falls as usual upon the rows and rows of old books,
the faded tawny-brown of the chair-covers, the one
rose and one orchid in their slim glasses on the
writing-table; and we blink up at grandfather
while he twinkles from his great height and displays
a pinch of something held between his finger and
thumb. He slips it into the keeping of the children,
share and share alike, as though it were a great
secret between us all, and we babble our gratitude
as well as we may. I always wished I could meet
that occasion, so often repeated, with less inco-
herence; for to have money in one's pocket is a
sensation that glorifies life, and it is hard to be
struck sheepish and awkward just as the prospect
opens so rosily. I bungled my thanks as usual—
but I dare say they showed plainly enough, while
I gaped at the difference that grandfather had made
in my outlook upon the world.

Then there was good-bye to be said to all the
members of the household; most important of all,
there was our last morning-visit to be paid to that
attic-room at the top of the house, where our perfect
old friend sat always patient and ready with her
love and welcome. We made our farewell to her
and she smiled tenderly—but these partings cost
her a few tears, and we left her sitting in her high-
backed arm-chair, among her innumerable relics and
keepsakes, beaming her blessing on us with speech-
less, shining looks. We knew that presently she
would insist on being helped into the passage outside her room, where there was a window that

overlooked the carriage-drive; she would be there for the moment of our departure, to wave a handkerchief as we drove away—she never failed. So we dashed downstairs again, the time now growing really short, and fled to the kitchen for a final gay exchange of good wishes with Mrs. Chapman—and up to the nursery once more, for tempestuous embraces of all our fond friends in order; and so yet again to the hall and the steps of the front-door, still with some minutes to wait, after all, till the carriage came sweeping round from the stables and Sidell pounded the gong and at last it was absolutely the moment to be off. Grandmother would be driving to the train with us, but grandfather stood in the great doorway, benevolently watching and smiling while Sidell packed us all into the carriage; and Patrick touched up the horses and the gravel crunched under our wheels and we craned about to answer the farewells thrown to us from the windows above—and sure enough there was a white handkerchief at the window of the top passage, high over all, which was the last we saw as we turned the corner and passed under the horse-chestnuts and up the drive towards the Norwich road. And only when we were out in the road and well on our journey came the exclamation of dismay (it always came in due course) from somebody of our party, " There now, I forgot—— " whatever it may have been, something of much importance; but it was too late to turn back, Earlham was far behind us already, our faces were set to the outer world.

You see, then, how all this stir and flutter of life, in prospect for the morrow, might affect us on our last evening at Earlham; it was like a freshening undertow beneath the stream of the smooth sweet hours. Bright as had been our weeks at Earlham, there was no melancholy over their end; there was only a livelier desire to cram the hours as full as they would hold, admitting nothing but the best. And if it should chance that this last evening was a Sunday, on the verge between summer and autumn, nothing could be better than the scene and the impression that I find there in the natural course, full in my path. Sunday evening, the pale light of the changing year, the stir of impending departure— it all brings me straight to the last of my pictures of memory, and this is one that crowns our long holiday to perfection. We had by now the sense of having lived with Earlham in deepest intimacy for an age; and yet there were always new dis- coveries to make in the regular round of the day, and we should prefer to keep jealously within it as the end approached. Nothing far-fetched or unlikely, but whatever most strictly belonged to the hour and the place, charged with the character of Earlham—this we desired; and my last picture is exactly the right one for our need. I find it before me, again in Earlham church.

16

By sundown the dusk was already grey in the body of the church, though up in the gallery there was still a flush and haze of warmth from the small west window of the tower. In the little north transept, in the chancel behind the dark carved screen, the shade deepened quickly; it began to be difficult to read one's book even before the psalms were at an end. No lamps were lit—there *were* none, I think; and perhaps this Sunday evening was reckoned as the last of the summer, and grandfather would announce that next week the hour of evening prayer must be shifted to the afternoon. I forget about that; but certainly the hurrying dusk of September overtook us; and only a few candles, a pair for the reading-desk, a pair for the Major, were lit when they were required, and their glimmering spots of light were all our illumination. The day held long enough for our needs, however, and we could lay aside our books in the twilight when grandfather mounted to the pulpit. Our particular corner of the chancel grew strange and solemn; it was a different place entirely from the cheerful and sociable enclosure where one studied the epitaphs in the morning. It was now full of awe—but of awe that in no way dismayed or oppressed, that rather sustained and encouraged a young spirit in its wordless answer to something larger than itself.

Our grandfather stood aloft in the pulpit, ghostly-white with his big surplice, remote and unfamiliar in the ebbing day. For us in the chancel the shine of the candle at his side outlined his clear profile— and his voice seemed to rise out of far-away distances, travelling through the falling night and reaching us across dim spaces where sight was lost. He was alone, up there in the candlelight; and the congregation, all motionless in the grey silence beneath him, left his solitude untouched. One listened to his voice, knowing and following exactly the curve of the well-known cadences; and yet it was strange, it was a voice from another sphere, and he himself, what with the glimmer and the shadow and the stillness, was changed, transfigured, exalted—one might never have seen him before. His preaching was like an appeal, an invocation that soared into the kindly night; and the thought that he uttered was as free and serene and unearthly as the night itself. God is a spirit—not a word that was spoken fell below that level of high imagination; the low earth of human littleness was left behind and forgotten. There was nothing in it all that a child might be supposed to understand; and a child accordingly, listening in a dream, scarcely heeding or apprehending a word, was brought without a check into the presence of a mind that could worship in spirit and in truth.

The sermon was long; but one forgets the weight of time in that twilit dream, floating upon space. Our grandfather preached without book or paper, and as his theme rose he too, I think, forgot the hour and was lost in the fervour of his vision. It was really as though he saw, as though he could catch a glimpse of a heaven that opened—and he broke out with an uncontrollable cry of admiration, pointing to the sight that brought healing to the world. Again and again it rang out; the revelation of hope was there, was suddenly before us for all to see—look, look and behold the promise fulfilled. He used no deliberate phrases; the word that leaps to the mouth is the only possible word, the only expressive, when the vision vouchsafed is always beyond expectation, rarer and lovelier than thought could foresee.   Again and again he called upon us to share the wonder ; and when he so called, it was not that he exhorted or adjured a faithless flock, crying out upon their blindness—there never was the least note of prophetic pride or indignation in his voice.   Humbly marvelling before the throne, joyful and thankful, he spoke of what he saw ; and though he spoke as one rapt to beatific heights, he had always a mild gravity of tone, he was simple and serious with the clarity of a fine understanding. A child who dreamily watched and listened to him, drinking in the impression, knew only that an evening hour in Earlham church was unlike any other in life.   But the quality of the hour, the taste of its beauty, was just as distinct to the child as to any of that company ; only the words to define it were wanting—if indeed they are not wanting as much as ever, even now.

Our grandmother, meanwhile, was beside us in our dim corner of the chancel ; she sat in her rightful place, close against the ancient oak screen— she slipped back to it as soon as the hymn had been sung and our grandfather crossed over to the pulpit ; and she sat there now, happy and quiet in the exaltation of her thought, with a look and touch of tenderness for the children at her side.   She too listened absorbed, and her eyes were lifted in a gaze that travelled away, above and beyond—away to the past of many memories, forward to the new morning and the reward of hope.   The words of the preacher dropped into her mind ; she took them, she made them her own, with a gentle movement of her head or the breathing of a sigh ; the stir of her

251

emotion was in the soft touch of her hand, as it
rested upon the child's hand in her lap. Half
smiling, half weeping out of a full heart, she raised
her face to the light that shone for her in the gathering darkness; she welcomed it with all the eager
faith of her being. The barriers that are about us
in the world, separating soul from soul, seemed to
be as nothing; and even the chasm that encircles
our small humanity, that isolates it in the midst
of the illimitable unknown, had vanished for an
hour—freely, freely our imprisoned thought could
escape to the truth beyond the stars. It seemed so,
there in the little shadowy church, while the few
scattered candles burnt brighter and whiter in the
gloom and the voice of the preacher sank gradually
to a hushed undertone, almost a whisper. The last
words were very quietly and intently breathed;
they hung and fell in the silence as lightly as a
falling leaf—another and another, more softly still,
and yet another, and it was the end. Stirring at
length and looking about us, we found that only the
very last of the twilight was left in the windows,
the night of autumn had all but closed us in.

There was still another hymn to be sung before
we dispersed; but our books were quite useless now,
and we waited while grandfather found the place
by the light of his candle and read out to us the
words of the first verse. He read them through, and
then the harmonium broke forth and we sang the
verse, all the congregation joining their voices with
fervent will. We paused, and grandfather read the
second verse; we took it up again, holding the
words in mind as well as we could—and so on to

252

the end. But indeed the words were most familiar, and in the evening and the gloom one sings more confidently than in the morning light; so that the successive verses of our hymn rolled out very heartily and everybody contributed his part. The children sang their loudest, Eliza lifted up her pillar of song in the gallery, a rich rumble of manly thunder arose from the village in the nave. We all felt a need of singing; in one way or another, clearly or obscurely, we had seen and known our portion in a high experience, an enhancement of power within, a disclosure of far distances; and a full tide of emotion was released, warm and buoyant, in the measured swing of the melody. But none of us sang as our grandmother sang—for the music she uttered, lightly throwing up her head, was alive with every thrill of her heart, it caught the very sparkle and shimmer of her loving, longing, adoring spirit. The words of the hymn were new upon her lips, so deep and sweet was the meaning with which she filled them; they seemed to be stirred, dignified, enlarged with all the sorrows and joys of a saintly life, that now was turning home towards the evening of its day. There was a passion of tenderness in her singing, there was thanksgiving and triumph; it was the voice of Christiana, stepping gladly down the last slope of the hill to the crossing of the river.

" Thy touch hath still its ancient power—no word from Thee can fruitless fall." Grandfather gave out the last lines of the hymn, closed his book, stood silent in the candlelight, while we threw ourselves once more into the music and swept to the climax. Our rhythm was broad and unhurried, our volume of sound moved steadily from beat to beat of the tune, mounting and descending. The few moments are enough for a long look, a glance that pierces the dimness and travels to and fro across the tiny church and seeks and finds—finds all that I have tried to speak of, all the images of memory that people the vision of our Earlham. It is a last look, and it fastens closely upon every light and shadow of the scene, scanning the rows of faces, passing between them to the more distant ghosts of the past, recovering the whole treasure of association that Earlham in its old age had amassed for its children. It was all there for the eyes that could see—all there in a moment of falling night, in the white shine of a few candle-flames, in a chorus of voices that hung upon the notes of a tune. Slowly, with gathering fervour, the voices lifted and rang out in the last words; and grandfather stood silent and tall, his head bowed, waiting for the close. " Hear, in this solemn evening hour—and in Thy mercy heal us all."

Printed in the United States
133398LV00002B/41/A